Ed Dudley, former PGA president,
in praise of

BEN HOGAN'S POWER GOLF:

"Take particular notice of what Ben Hogan
has to say about getting distance. While he
weighs only 137 pounds, Ben is one of the
longest hitters the game has ever known,
comparing very favorably in this department
to many men of more muscular physique.

"Hogan gets his distance by making
considerable use of his body. His hand action
at the moment of impact with the ball is
terrific.

"Don't get the idea, however, that Ben has
any weaknesses in the other departments of the
game. He would never have won so many
events on such a variety of courses without
having a full bag of tricks. What's more, he
does a good job of telling you how he
does it in this book."

Ben Hogan's

POWER
GOLF

PUBLISHED BY POCKET BOOKS NEW YORK

ACKNOWLEDGMENTS

To Ed Dudley for so kindly providing the Foreword.

To MacGregor Golf, Inc., for their cooperation and advice.

To Cliff Roberts, Bob Jones and the other members of the Augusta, Georgia, National Golf Club for their kind permission to use their course as the background for the pictures used to illustrate the original edition of this book.

To Tony Sheehan of Augusta, Georgia, for his patience, enthusiasm and exhaustive efforts to provide the best possible photographs [from which the line drawings in this book were sketched] that could be made to use in illustrating this book.

POCKET BOOKS, a Simon & Schuster division of
GULF & WESTERN CORPORATION
1230 Avenue of the Americas, New York, N.Y. 10020

ISBN: 0-671-46988-6

First Pocket Books printing April, 1953

25   24   23   22   21   20

POCKET and colophon are registered trademarks
of Simon & Schuster.

Printed in the U.S.A.

Dedication

To HENRY PICARD

Champion, Professional Golfers Association, 1939

ONE of the best friends I have in professional golf is Henry Picard, an outstanding player, an outstanding teacher and an outstanding man. As most of you know, when I first started playing tournament golf I didn't do too well. It was a long time before I won enough money to pay my expenses. Although Picard was probably unaware of it at the time, I can truthfully say now that the encouragement and an offer of financial assistance that I received from Henry at one very important period in my golfing career gave me the courage to keep going.

This story will probably embarrass Henry, but it is so typical of him that I would like to tell it anyhow and I hope he will forgive me. At one time during those early days before I had ever won a tournament my finances were low and I was a long way from home.

In fact, I had no idea of where the money was going to come from to get my wife and me home in case I didn't win any in the particular tournament I was playing in at the time. Henry must have sensed my predicament because he came to me before that tournament and said, "Look, Ben, I don't know what your financial situation is and it is none of my business, but I want you to know that if you ever need any help to stay on the tour you can always come to me."

Fortunately, I never did have to call on Picard for financial assistance. But knowing that help was there if I needed it enabled me to forget abut my troubles. I went out and won enough money in that tournament to keep going. I've been going ever since.

Again, when he decided that he wanted to play tournament golf only occasionally, Henry recommended me for the job that he held as the playing professional for the Hershey, Pennsylvania, Country Club. Thanks to Henry's recommendation I got the job. For some years I represented Hershey on the tournament tour and it was a very pleasant association for me.

To sum it all up, Picard by his offers of financial assistance, his recommendation, words of encouragement and golfing hints, has helped me more than I can ever repay. Never in all the years that I have known him have I ever been able to repay him for his interest in me.

Therefore, as a small measure of gratitude and appreciation, I would like to dedicate this book to Henry Picard. He has been a real friend and an inspiration to me at all times.

Foreword

By ED DUDLEY

Former President, Professional Golfers Association

HAVING watched the thoroughness and patience with which Ben Hogan went about making himself an outstanding golfer, I welcomed the invitation to write this Foreword for his golf book. I was sure that any golf book with Ben's name on it would be a thorough job. And this book is no disappointment.

Few golfers have worked harder or have had to overcome more handicaps to become outstanding. Watching Ben Hogan play now it is hard to believe that such a smooth golfing machine started left-handed, shifted over to play from the right side but cross-handed and then tried both the conventional right-handed interlocking and overlapping grips before he finally settled upon an adaptation of the overlapping grip which he uses today as a solution to his problems in that department of the game.

During the war Bobby Jones played with Hogan in a big tournament in Chicago. Afterward he told Grantland Rice and me, "I thought I was a hard worker at this game. I thought Hagen and Sarazen were hard workers. But Ben Hogan is the hardest worker I've ever seen, not only in golf, but in any other sport.

"I've taken my share of beating," said Bobby. "So have all the others. But no one has ever taken the beating Hogan takes. He thinks only in terms of birdies. Several times out there he was actually trying to hole out a sixty or seventy yard pitch. His goal is never the green. It's the cup. And you can say that ability to take punishment is a big part of winning golf."

When Ben Hogan first appeared on the tournament circuit I was playing in tournaments regularly myself. I've seen Ben miss a two-iron shot and then after that round take his caddy and go out on the practice tee and practice for hours at a time nothing but similar shots to the one he missed.

That thoroughly studious approach to the game is not only reflected in his own swing, but also in the knowledge of the finer points of golf which he discusses in this book. On his way to the top Ben experimented with every phase of the golf swing and he is fully aware of what he is doing at all times.

Hogan won his first major championship when he captured the PGA Championship at Portland, Oregon, in 1946. It's a cinch that it won't be his last because he has been a consistent winner since 1938, leading the money winners in 1940, 1941, 1942 and 1946, and he was just about reaching his peak of form in 1942 when he entered the Army Air Corps. Service in the Army, however, has only delayed his claim to fame as a winner of major championships which he proved when he won at Portland.

Take particular notice of what Ben Hogan has to say about getting distance. While he only weighs approximately 137 pounds, Ben is one of the longest hitters the game has ever known, comparing very favorably in this department to many men of more muscular physique.

Hogan gets his distance by making considerable use of his body. His hand action at the moment of impact with the ball is terrific.

Don't get the idea, however, that Ben has any weaknesses in the other departments of the game. He never would have won so many events on such a variety of courses without having a full bag of tricks. What's more, he does a good job of telling you how he does it in this book.

Contents

ACKNOWLEDGMENTS   iv

DEDICATION   v

FOREWORD   vii

INTRODUCTION   xi

CHAPTER

I	Evolution of the Hogan Grip	1
II	Clubs . . . Selection and Use	13
III	Stance Gives You Balance	20
IV	The Full Swing	35
	The Backswing	35
	The Downswing	38
V	Turning on the Power	57
	Wood Shots for Distance	59
VI	Iron Shots for Accuracy	82
	Pitch and Chip Shots	87
	Variations	90
VII	Putting	136
VIII	Bunker Shots Are Easy	145
IX	Uphill and Downhill Shots	158
X	Stormy Weather Golf	163
	Rain and Storm	163
	Wind Shots	165
XI	Now, It's Up to You	169
	Match Play Golf	174
	Eight Hints on How To Lower Your Score	177

Introduction

CONTRARY to anything you may have read on the subject, there is no such individual as a born golfer. Some have more natural ability than others, but they've all been made.

What I would like to do through the medium of this golf book is to improve your swing and cut a few strokes off your score. In order for me to accomplish this you must be willing to do a little thinking and a lot of work.

During the course of this book I am going to make available to you the things I have learned about golf in the hours I have spent on the practice tee, and in the tournaments in which I have played. Developing a golf swing is not impossible. There are those who would have you believe that, but it is not so.

However, in order to develop a golf swing your thoughts must run in the right direction. Otherwise it will be impossible. Perhaps you will understand me better when I say that when you grip a golf club to take your first swing at a golf ball every natural instinct you employ to accomplish that objective is wrong, absolutely wrong.

Reverse every natural instinct you have and do just the opposite of what you are inclined to do and you will probably come very close to having a perfect golf swing. However, every golfer, even the so-called "natural player," learns the hard way. Some are just a little more fortunate than others in being able to learn a little quicker, that's all.

My approach to golf in this book will be positive rather than negative. In other words, you will not read anything in this book which will make you self-conscious and frighten you by emphasizing all of the faults you can acquire in trying to develop a golf swing.

While I am approaching golf instruction from the positive rather than the negative side I plan to tell you the whys and wherefores for everything I ask you to do. In that connection I want to emphasize that there is a perfectly good reason for everything I do in playing golf, a reason arrived at by constant application of the trial-and-error method.

Nor do I overemphasize my experiences along those lines. As you will be aware, after reading the chapter in this book on the evolution of my grip, there isn't a mistake I haven't made while trying to learn to play golf.

I have been asked if I think a novice could learn to play golf from a book. Of course, the best way to learn to play golf is from a competent instructor. There is no denying that. But I am convinced that if you follow the suggestions that I make in this book closely, and give them a lot of thought and attention when you are practicing and playing, they will help you cut down on your scores. How many strokes will be cut off your total depends upon you as an individual.

Golf scores, however, are relative. In my opinion the greatest rounds of golf are not shot by the tournament professionals and hot-shot amateurs, but by the 85-90 shooters. That may seem like an exaggerated statement, but I honestly believe it to be true and I'll tell you why.

The lowest score ever made by a professional in competition is 62. Several of us are co-holders of that record. I have shot two rounds of 62, one at Oakland, California, and another at Chicago, Illinois. Walter Hagen, Lawson Little, Byron Nelson, Jimmy Demaret, Jim Ferrier and Herman Keiser are the other professionals who have had 62's in competition.

Any time you can shoot a 62, no matter how easy the

course may be, that's great golf. But to my mind any time an 85-90 golfer shoots a 75, that's even greater golf.

That is the equivalent of a professional shooting a 59. It is a fair comparison because it is impossible for the 85-90 golfers to reach the green at half the holes in two strokes on most courses.

When they do reach the green in two they have to take a wood club to do it, but we can accomplish the same thing with a short iron. Shooting at a green with a wood club gives them a much smaller target to shoot at than we have when we use an iron.

That's because it is almost impossible for the 85-90 shooters to hit the green with a wood shot and still hold the ball on it. Whereas, we can put plenty of bite on the ball with our short irons and it stays on the green almost where we want it.

It would discourage me if I had to play a golf course the way most 85-90 shooters have to play it. They know they have very little chance of staying on the greens, but they let fly at them with their wood clubs anyhow.

They are hoping that the ball will stay on the green if they are lucky enough to hit a straight shot. That is next to impossible, even if they hit it straight, because the ball comes into the green off a wood club with lots of speed and with very little bite on it.

As a contrast, we play the ball high or low, according to the problem confronting us, and with plenty of bite on it.

The way most golf courses are trapped the 85-90 golfers have to shoot around a bunker from the tee. We don't give the ordinary bunker a thought because we can drive over most of them with no bother at all.

My hat is off to the plus 85 shooters. Those are the fellows I want to help with this book. If they still retain their enthusiasm for the game considering the way they have to play it, then they deserve any help I can give them.

Bobby Jones once very aptly expressed what I think is the ideal philosophy behind the normal golfer's desire to play the game well when he said, "If golf is worth playing at all, it's worth playing right."

Of course, this book isn't going to make another Jones out of you, but I think it might help to make you what I would describe as a social golfer. Someone once estimated that 90 is the dividing line between a golfer and a dub. If that is true, then only about 15 to 20% of those who play the game can accurately describe themselves as golfers.

Fortunately, the percentage of those who think of themselves as golfers is much higher than that. If you have the idea that you can learn to play golf, then you have something to start with and you'll probably find the answer to a good many of your problems in this book.

BEN HOGAN

CHAPTER I

Evolution of the Hogan Grip

MANY golf fans are surprised to learn that I played golf left-handed when I first took up the game. Mention of that fact in the golf column I write for the newspapers attracted a flock of letters. Right away many left-handed golfers interpreted the fact that I now play right-handed to mean that I was of the opinion that all left-handed players should play the game from the right side, that golf is a one-sided game. But that isn't so at all.

There is absolutely no reason why anybody should change over from playing golf left-handed and start learning the game all over again from the right side. Particularly now that left-handed clubs are made just as well as right-handed clubs and are as comparatively easy to get as right-handed clubs.

I changed over when I was a small boy. The only clubs I could get were right-handed clubs. Moreover, most of the fellows I played with then were very convincing in telling me that left-handers never made good golfers. At that age I was gullible enough to believe them and to make the change, but I wouldn't be now.

There are many more good right-handed golfers than there are left-handed players, of course, but that's merely a matter of percentages. There are many more right-handed players than there are those who play the game from the left side.

Certainly the designs of golf courses are no disadvan-

tage to left-handed players. There are just as many dog-
legs to the left as to the right.

Those left-handed golfers who wrote in to ask if they
should change over and play right-handed probably
wouldn't have written in had they known the story of the
evolution of my grip. In that connection let me say that I
have tried all of the grips known to golfers at some time
or another in my career.

The grip I now use was arrived at by a series of trial-
and-error experiments which began when I first took up
the game. As recently as the fall of 1945, when I got out
of the service, I made a radical change in my grip which
I had been experimenting with whenever I got a chance
to play golf while in the Army.

I had been aware for some time that if I wanted to
make a comeback as a successful golfer after I was dis-
charged from the Army that I would have to make a
change in my grip to correct a tendency I had always had
to overswing on the backswing. By the time I resumed
tournament play I had made the change and had everything in good working order.

Formerly I used a grip in which I had what might be
best described as a long thumb when speaking of the
position of the thumb of the left hand on the shaft. During
the course of the backswing that thumb used to slide
down on the shaft and as a result I was always guilty of
a certain looseness at the top of my swing which pre-
vented me from getting the maximum of control.

In correcting this I pushed the left thumb back up on
the shaft. The entire change couldn't have amounted to
more than half an inch in the movement of the thumb,
but it was enough to restrict my backswing so that it no
longer is loose.

To the novice that one-half-inch shift of the thumb
position won't seem much of a change, but just how
radical a change it was can be gathered from the fact
that my friends among the pros spotted it the minute I
resumed tournament golf and commented on it. All of
which should impress upon you the importance of the
grip in relation to the golf swing. It also should give you

a good idea of how closely the tournament professionals watch one another for ideas.

It took me some time to get accustomed to that new grip, but as I said before I had it in working order when I resumed tournament play in 1945. I made my first start with it at Knoxville, Tennessee, that fall and while I didn't expect it to function efficiently under the stress of tournament play I surprised myself by shooting a 287 for the 72 holes, which was good enough to collect third money. I was well satisfied with the way the new grip had stood up under its baptism of competitive fire and I've used it ever since.

The nearest publicized grip to which my grip can be compared is the overlapping grip made famous by Harry Vardon, the great English player, and adopted by so many top players in this country. Strictly speaking, however, my grip is not the same.

My grip differs from the conventional overlapping grip in the relationship between the little fingers of the right hand to the index finger of the left hand and the position of my right hand on my left.

In the conventional overlapping grip the little finger of the right hand overlaps the index finger of the left hand. Whereas I have found that I am able to get a firmer grip, transmitting more power to the clubhead, by gripping the little finger of my right hand around the knob of the knuckle of the index finger of my left hand.

My grip also differs from that of other golfers in that my right hand rides higher on the outside of my left hand. This enables the two hands to act as a single unit, thus imparting considerably more hand action and consequently more clubhead speed at the moment of impact.

Getting the proper grip at the start is one of the most important steps in learning how to play golf. For that reason let us first consider the intents and purposes of the grip in relation to golf.

One reason why the grip is so important is because by means of it we telegraph our energy and our desires to the club. To do this with a maximum amount of efficiency we've got to have a grip which will permit our hands and wrists to work properly as one unit and not against each other.

The idea is to have free and uniform hand action throughout the swing while still maintaining the clubface at the proper angle when it strikes the ball. The objective is to make a solid contact of the clubhead with the ball at the exact moment you are telegraphing your greatest amount of energy to the club via the grip.

In taking up the grip it always seemed to me a good idea to have the clubhead resting in its natural position on the ground just as you would like to have it hit the ball. Doing this as you take up your grip will insure you of a reasonable chance that the clubface will be in that position when it makes contact with the ball during the course of the swing.

In connection with any discussion of the grip one question which I am asked quite frequently is, "Do you exercise your hands?" The answer is that I do, but not as much as when I wasn't able to play as much as I am playing right now. The condition of your hands is very important and if you don't get a chance to play often it is a good idea to exercise your hands and keep them in condition.

Your hands must be strong and yet at the same time sensitive to the demands put on them. They must be strong and at the same time have a delicate touch because there are shots in golf which require the finesse and touch of a master billiard player if you are going to pull them off when they will mean the most to you.

Personally, I like my hands to be thin. When they feel puffy I can't grip the club the way I like to. I can't explain why, but some mornings my hands will feel fat and puffy. When they feel that way I know that I am not going to play my best that day. Which should give you an idea of the relation of the condition of your hands to successful golf.

To exercise my hands I take a towel and squeeze it with both hands until my forearms are good and hard. However, I don't exercise my hands unless I have been forced to lay off golf. Most of the time I play enough to keep my hands fit without exercising them. Nor do I find it necessary to wear a glove while playing.

Special exercises for the hands are good, but don't over-do them. Don't make the mistake a well-known professional did while on his way to the 1937 National Open Championship at Cherry Hills in Denver, Colorado. Traveling by train, he decided that he would keep his hands in shape during the train ride by special exercise and so he bought a hard rubber ball. All of the way out to Colorado he kept working with that ball, squeezing it and then relaxing his grip. He repeated the process over and over again. But when the morning of the first round of the tournament arrived he couldn't control a shot. He had lost that sense of "feel" in his hands which is essential to tournament golf. That was a mighty expensive experiment in special exercises for that particular professional.

As I favor my own version of the overlapping grip, naturally that's the one I am going to talk about in this book. Starting with the left hand, my grip is very definitely a palm grip. The leather or rubber grip on the shaft of your club will lie diagonally across the palm of the left hand just above the callus pad.

In folding the left hand around the club the left thumb will be slightly on the right side of the shaft. As you look down on your left hand in gripping the club you should be able to see the first three finger joints on the outside of that hand. It also should be apparent to you that your left hand is well over the shaft.

In gripping with the left hand there is definitely more pressure on the last three fingers of that hand than there is on the index finger and thumb. While gripping with these three fingers you should also push down on the top of the leather or rubber grip of your club with the butt of your hand. This will assure you of a firm grip. Try it and you will get the sensation of having the club locked in that hand.

As far as the right hand is concerned my grip is definitely a finger grip. By that I mean that the club lies diagonally across the fingers of the right hand below the callus pad. When you fold the right hand over the grip

on the shaft you will find that if you have gripped the
club correctly there is a cup formed in the palm of the
hand that will allow space enough for the left thumb.
The thumb of the right hand is slightly on the left side
of the shaft and not on the top.

Make sure that the right hand rides high on the left
hand. The purpose of this, of course, is to mold the two
hands together so that they can act as one unit and not
two. The greatest pressure in the right hand is in the two
middle fingers. That is because the club is well down in
the fingers of the right hand with a lot of hand left over.

VARIATIONS

No novice golfer should experiment with his grip, but
when your scores testify as to your progress there are a
couple of slight changes which you can make in your
grip which will enable you to hook or slice at will. You
will find an ability to hook or slice on purpose will be
convenient for you because you will then be able to play
around some of the obstacles which may confront you
on the golf course.

Remember, however, that these tips are for the more
advanced players. The novice should not experiment until
he has the fundamentals down pat. He should wait until
he can hit the ball straight consistently before he starts
fooling around with his grip.

If you want to hook a ball turn both hands toward the
right side on the grip or shaft. This position should feel
sort of unnatural and should permit you to hook the ball
without altering your golf swing.

The reason you assume this grip for a hook shot is
because your hands will come back to the normal position
while in the process of the swing and will automatically
close the face of the club at impact, assuring you of the
desired hook.

To play a slice, or just the reverse of a hook shot, the
grip should be altered to the left. Turn both hands toward the left over the shaft.

With the grip thus adjusted the hands will assume

the natural position through the normal processes of the swing. This will open the face of the club, giving you the desired fade or slice.

Let me warn you, however, that in taking up the grip for either the hook or the slice be sure that the face of your club is square to the line of flight. Don't just turn the club. When you decide to play a hook or a slice be sure to loosen your grip and regrip the club for the shot you desire to make.

Both the hook and the slice are handy shots to have in your bag of tricks. But only if you hook or slice with preconceived intent.

Learning to hook and slice on purpose and with control should give you an idea of what makes the ball take either line of flight. When you acquire that knowledge a hook or slice should cause you no more concern.

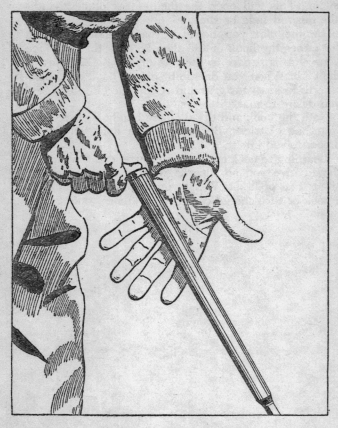

The club in the left hand runs diagonally across the palm. Although it is hard to see in this picture because it shadows the palm calluses, the club is actually above these calluses and below the butt pad of my hand, running diagonally across the palm down into the forefinger.

In folding the left hand around the club the thumb of my left hand is slightly on the right side of the shaft. Looking down on my left hand I can easily see the first three hand-knuckle joints. Also note that my left hand is well over the shaft. The V formed between the index finger and the thumb points approximately over my right shoulder.

The club lies diagonally across the fingers of my right hand below the callus pad. Take note of where the butt of my right hand is in relation to the left hand before it is folded over.

This picture clearly shows that the grip in my right hand is definitely in the fingers. The little finger of my right hand is hooked back of the knuckle of the index finger of my left hand.

In folding my right hand over there is a cup formed which allows space enough for the left thumb. The thumb of my right hand is slightly on the left side of the shaft. The V formed between the index finger and thumb of my right hand is in line with the shaft.

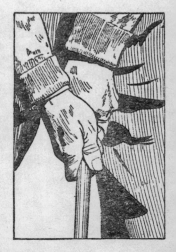

My right hand rides very high on the left hand in my grip. The purpose in doing this is to mold the hands together so they act as one unit. The greatest pressure in my right hand is in the middle two fingers.

This view of my grip with the knuckles showing reveals the position of the fingers in relation to each other. It is an excellent illustration of how I wrap the little finger of my right hand across the index finger of my left hand and around the knuckle. This is a grip adjustment of my own. Used, I believe, only by me. It makes for a firmer grip at all times during the swing and as a result I can propel the club much faster while still having maximum use of my wrists.

Hook Grip. To hook ball turn both hands toward the right side as I have done here. It will feel unnatural, but it will enable you to hook without altering your swing. Your hands come back to a normal position while you swing and automatically close the face of the club at impact, insuring a hook.

Slice Grip. Here I have turned the hands over toward the left over the shaft. During the swing they come back to a normal position, automatically opening the face of the club and giving the desired fade or slice. In assuming any grip the club-face should be square to the line of flight. When gripping the club to play a slice or hook be sure to loosen your hands and regrip, placing them in the desired position.

CHAPTER II

Clubs...Selection and Use

ALL golfers are alike in one respect. They are always on the lookout for new clubs. That is why the average golfer never goes into a golf shop without feeling and testing almost every club he can put his hands on, even if he has no fault to find with the clubs he is using.

He just wants to be prepared for the day when his favorite clubs wear out or break. He won't feel so bad when that happens if he has the replacements in his locker.

In selecting clubs I always look for those which suit my swing. I've spent too long developing that swing to make any radical changes in it merely to fit a new club.

Maybe you'll get the idea of how important it is to get clubs which "feel" right if I recite a few of my own experiences looking for replacements. While playing in the Pro-Amateur Tournament which preceded the 1947 Phoenix, Arizona, Open, I broke my favorite driver. I had used it constantly since 1937 and during that time I won more than my share of prize money with it. Although I am now using another driver I wouldn't say that as yet I have found a club which has replaced the old one in my affections.

The only comparison I can make of the difference between golf clubs is to say that playing with a new club is something like breaking in a new pair of shoes. However, I have found it a lot easier to find a new pair of shoes that I like than I have to find a new driver.

Long before I broke that driver I was looking for one that felt as good to me. I knew that it wasn't going to last forever because of the hard and constant use I give my clubs, but I wasn't lucky enough to find a replacement.

Any time I discuss clubs I am always asked, "How much does your driver weigh?" and "How long is it?" That is because most golfing fans are interested in learning how to drive for distance. And for some reason they think that the secret of how tournament golfers get such tremendous distances off the tee must be wrapped up in their drivers.

Making any set rule on the length or weight of the driver for you to use, without fitting it to your individual needs, would be an error. The old golf instructional theory used to be that a short man should use a short club and a tall man should use a long club, but students of the game have come to realize that the reverse is nearer to the correct theory.

For instance, Bobby Cruickshank, who is only slightly more than five feet in height and is always referred to as "The Wee Scot," uses a driver with a 44-inch shaft.

Manufacturers, however, have standardized the length and weight of clubs. The standard length of the driver is 43 inches. The weight of my wood clubs is 14 ounces each, but 13¼ to 13½ ounces seems to be a good weight for the average player.

In selecting your driver it would be foolish for you to pick a club with a lot of whip if you have a short, fast backswing because you would have trouble controlling it. If you are older and have a full, slow swing you should use a club with enough flex in the shaft so that you can feel the clubhead.

The weight of the clubhead should also be in relation to the flex of the shaft. If you have a stiff, heavy shaft your club has to have more weight in the clubhead in order for you to get the "feel" of the clubhead during the swing. The lighter and more flexible the shaft, the less weight needed in the clubhead.

In selecting and using your wood clubs it would be well for you to remember that sometimes a player can change clubheads without getting into difficulty, but generally speaking he is asking for trouble when he changes the shafts. The reason is that the flex and the weight of all shafts are different and they have a direct effect on the swing.

In regard to the clubhead and its function, most golf fans don't realize that during the course of the ideal golf swing the clubhead is ahead of the shaft as you approach the ball. Until moving pictures showed exactly what was taking place most people imagined that the clubhead was behind the shaft.

If there is any difference in the flex of the shaft from what you are accustomed to, no matter how slight, it can throw your swing off. Most long hitters prefer stiff shafts to whippy ones. The fast swingers are not always the long hitters. Give a lot of consideration to the relationship of the flex of the shaft to your swing before you select your wood clubs.

While iron clubs are turned out on precision machinery it is not always easy to find an iron that "feels" right. During the 1946 National Open Championship at the Canterbury Country Club in Cleveland, Ohio, for instance, my nine iron was either lost or stolen. I've never been able to find a nine iron since which "feels" as good to me as my old one.

Putting is probably the least standardized phase of the game of golf and golfers are just as individual in the selection of their putters as they are in their styles of putting. More weird-looking putters are sold at the average golf shop than any other type of club. Since putting is such an individual art, nobody has been able to prove that you can improve your efficiency by standardizing the instrument used.

As for my own preference in putters, I am always on the lookout for one that sets straight away. They're not as easy to find as you might imagine. In fact, I haven't seen more than five putters in my life that, when examined closely, weren't hooked.

Lest you begin to suspect that I am a bit of an old woman about my clubs let me say that club "feel" was even important to Bobby Jones. Upon his retirement the clubs that Jones had used in winning his many championships were tested scientifically for center of gravity, moments of inertia, etc. Bobby's clubs, which were hickory shafted and which he laboriously acquired one by one over the years, were actually a perfect match with the exception of his mashie niblick, which would be known as the eight iron today.

"I always had trouble with that club," was Jones' comment when informed of the result of the tests.

Now that you have some idea of what to look for in selecting your clubs, let's give some consideration to what club to use when faced with a shot. Naturally, this is governed to some extent by individual ability, but there are certain things which I can tell you here which will be of help to you.

Your club selection for a shot should be governed by the amount of loft required in the flight of the ball and the distance it is to travel. The more loft to the clubface the easier it is to hit a straight ball.

The amount of confidence you have in your ability to play a particular club should also be given some consideration when you are selecting a club to make a shot which appears to be difficult. You can substitute a club you favor for the correct club to be used on a particular shot only if your favorite is quite similar to the correct club in the loft of its clubface.

When addressing the ball make sure that the clubhead is resting with its entire bottom surface on the ground. Also check to make sure that the bottom edge of the clubface is at right angles to the intended line of flight. In order to play any shot correctly the lie of the clubhead must be entirely on the ground and yet permit you to take up a comfortable position as you stand up to the ball. If it doesn't, your whole swing will be off or the clubface may be twisted out of its proper striking position at the moment of contact.

In selecting any club to make a shot it is well to have

an idea of its relation to the distance confronting you. Of course, no matter whether they are using woods or irons, no two players will necessarily use precisely the same club for precisely the same distance.

That's because there is a matter of personal adjustment which comes into play. The particular range of any club should be adapted to suit the strength of the player. Then, again, some players have a tendency to loft the ball more easily than others. In which case they will use a longer iron to get the same distance as the player who doesn't get as much loft.

From:	Regular	Maximum	Minimum
Driver	265	300	235
Brassie	250	270	220
Three Wood	235	250	210
Four Wood	220	230	200
One Iron	195	220	185
Two Iron	185	210	175
Three Iron	175	200	165
Four Iron	165	190	155
Five Iron	155	180	145
Six Iron	145	170	135
Seven Iron	135	160	125
Eight Iron	125	150	115
Nine Iron	115	140	105
Wedge (Pitch)	50 in	105	in to green
Wedge (Sand)	25	40	in to green

The preceding table is my graded list of distances for the various clubs. You will have to find your own distances, of course, but I have graded my clubs according to regular, maximum and minimum distances to give you some idea of the ratio between clubs.

Naturally, weather conditions will alter all maximums and minimums. These gradings are based on ideal weather conditions, but heavier air will make it more difficult for you to get distance. On a heavy day subtract approximately ten yards from each club.

Another factor to be considered is the condition of the fairways. Hard fairways will give you more roll. Soft fairways will stop the ball from rolling.

If there is one club in the bag neglected by novices and duffers, it is the sand wedge. In fact, most novices don't even have a sand wedge in their bags.

That ignorance of the value of a sand wedge probably isn't as strange as it seems to me. Dai Rees and Charley Ward, the two English professionals who played in our tournaments during the winter of 1946-1947, marveled at the way American professionals have mastered the use of the sand wedge. They said that if they hadn't learned anything else during their tour, the trip was worth while just because of what they learned about using this club.

"Most English players don't even use the sand wedge," said Rees when I talked about it with him. "They don't know its value."

Too bad they don't, however, because a sand wedge, if anyone will take the trouble to learn how to use it, can be the most useful club in the kit.

Even when a duffer does buy a sand wedge he usually buys the wrong kind. He should select a sand wedge with a wide flange on the sole of the club. This flange on the underside of the clubhead prevents the blade from digging into the ground too deep.

When you set the club down on a flat surface the flange should be at an angle so that the back of the flange will hold the leading edge of the face of the club up off the surface approximately one quarter of an inch.

Most golfers don't realize that the use of the sand wedge is not restricted to sand traps or bunkers. It is ideal, for instance, to use on pitch shots.

In using the sand wedge to make a pitch shot all you have to do is to hit a little back of the ball. This club is ideal for pitch shots because the blade has plenty of loft and the flange prevents the club blade from digging into the ground. When this shot is gauged correctly and hit properly the ball should fly right up and give you the correct loft for a pitch shot to the green.

Experiment with this club a little to find what your maximum distance with it is. After you have determined your maximum you can go ahead and start using it for all pitch shots from your maximum distance right on in to the green.

Furthermore, it is an ideal club to use when you want the ball to stop suddenly after it lands. In order to get the most efficient use out of this club, however, you must spend a little time practicing with it. But it's worth it as proficiency with the sand wedge will pay dividends.

While the United States Golf Association restricts the number of clubs to fourteen most professionals use sixteen in all tournaments except USGA sponsored events and the Masters' Tournament, which is also a fourteen club affair. When I compete in a tournament in which the number of clubs is restricted I make my selection on the basis of the clubs which will be the most useful to me during that particular tournament.

For instance, during the 1947 Masters' Tournament at Augusta, Georgia, I left my double-duty niblick in my locker. But before the tournament I spent a good deal of time practicing chipping with my sand wedge in order to make up for the absence of that particular club from my bag.

In conclusion let me say that you'll strengthen your game considerably if you become more familiar with all of the clubs in your bag. No matter what situation confronts you during the course of a round you will at least know what club to use if you know what each club is for, and how it should be played.

CHAPTER III

Stance Gives You Balance

THE foot movements of a high-class player during the course of his swing are made so quickly and smoothly that they quite often are taken for granted by everybody except the most observant student of the game. It is possible to play good golf from the hips upwards, but you must have good form from the hips down to be a really first-class player.

Those who are observant enough to notice the footwork of the top players will come to realize that balance is an important part of every golf shot. They will realize also that it is impossible to attain balance without the proper foot action during the course of the swing.

There is more involved in the correct stance than positions of the feet. When I have taken up what I consider the ideal position for hitting a golf ball I feel as though I were a tripod with my two feet and the clubhead as the three points of contact with the ground.

While that is the best comparison I can think of to describe my position at the ball, it isn't entirely correct. The weight of a tripod is evenly distributed between its three points of contact with the ground, but in the ideal position at the ball the weight is evenly distributed between both feet.

None of your weight should rest on the clubhead point of contact. That will be true if the weight is back through the heel as it should be. You should never feel that the weight is forward on your feet if you have taken up the correct position.

When you look at the ideal golf posture from the rear the most noticeable feature is the prominence of the golfer's posterior. The *derrière,* if I may use the name women's fashion magazines have for it, definitely protrudes.

Yet at the same time the line from the waist up to the back of the head is a straight one. There should be no bend or curve to the back.

Both knees should be flexed at all times. What's more, they swing in toward one another. This bending, however, isn't exaggerated. You shouldn't feel that you are knock-kneed, for instance.

This position should give you the feel that you possess a firm foundation which at the same time permits you a freedom of movement in your shoulders, hips and arms. There should be nothing in your position at the ball to prevent you from keeping perfect balance at all times and having a free swing.

Most beginners don't take the time to set themselves up at the ball with the correct stance. The idea is to get a good firm grip on the ground and yet not be rooted there. Strong and supple legs are just as important to good golf as strong and supple arms and wrists.

Another common mistake among beginning golfers is that they stand too far away from the ball during the address. Yet in the ideal position you should feel that you are away from the ball rather than over the top of it. You can avoid the feeling of being over the ball by not curving your back from the waist as I have described above.

There is some confusion in the minds of many golfers as to the relationship between the positions of the feet and the various clubs.

Whenever I discuss the stance with a golfer he will invariably ask, "How far apart are the feet?" There is no way that I can tell you exactly how many inches apart your feet should be for the various clubs because that is something which varies with the individual.

Actually, there are sixteen positions for the feet. Or

as many positions as there are clubs in your bag. Beyond giving you a few general hints as to how to go about finding out what they are, as far as you are concerned there is nothing I can tell you which will solve this problem. It has to be worked out by the trial-and-error method.

The type of stance you take on any shot should insure good balance, be comfortable and provide a good firm footing. You should be anchored firmly to the ground, but at the same time be able to make an easy shift of the weight to the right leg going back.

There are three basic stances. The others are variations of these according to the club being used on the shot.

The basic stances are the square, the closed and the open. In the square stance both feet are equidistant from an imaginary line which should parallel the intended line of flight. In the open stance your left foot is slightly withdrawn from the imaginary line parallel to the intended line of flight. For a closed stance your right foot is dropped back slightly from the imaginary line parallel to the intended line of flight.

Whatever stance you use, however, take a comfortable position opposite the ball. The weight is evenly distributed between both feet. The weight on each foot is back through the heel from the ball. You should never feel that the weight is forward on your feet.

Place the feet so that a line across the toes would parallel the intended line of flight. Turn the toes outward slightly. The distance between the feet is determined by the type of shot being made.

Let me caution you not to make the mistake many golfers make of using a stance that is too wide. There is a definite tendency on the part of novice golfers to place the feet too far apart.

This has the effect of restricting the hip turn in both directions. The best way to measure your stance is to place your feet apart about a little less than the width of your shoulders for the square stance, used for a five iron shot, and make your adjustments and variations from there. Turning the toes of both feet slightly outward will also aid you in making an unrestricted turn during the swing.

Perhaps you will understand the relationship between the positions of the feet and the clubs if I start by explaining the positions of the feet for short iron shots. A good key to the variation of your stance in iron play is to remember that as the numbers of your irons increase, one, two, three, etc., the width of your stance decreases and also opens.

The five iron is the dividing iron between short irons and long irons and most of the top players use a slightly opened stance for the short irons up to the five iron. From there on up through the long irons, the four, three, two and one, however, the stance increases in width and becomes squarer.

In taking up your positions to play the short irons the feet are fairly close together. The left foot is withdrawn slightly from the imaginary line parallel to the line of flight, forming the open stance.

The left toe is pointed out and the hips have been faced slightly toward the objective. The weight is equally distributed between both feet. The knees are flexed and bent in toward each other slightly.

This stance is used on short iron shots because it enables you to keep your left side out of the way while contacting the ball and going on through the follow-through to the finish. The reason is that the swing is so short that it is impossible to take a full turn with the hips to accommodate the hands and arms with space to swing through.

The stance I favor for long irons, fairway wood clubs and the driver is a closed stance, particularly for the fairway wood clubs and the driver. The reason is that this stance gives you more traction and balance. It enables you to strike the more powerful blow required to get the most out of those clubs. In order to get real distance with them you've got to be firmly anchored.

Another reason for favoring this stance on these shots is that it enables you to turn your body more freely. Freedom of body turn permits you to lengthen the arc of your swing for the longer shots.

Remember to turn both toes out slightly. This will aid you to keep your balance during the full swing and at the same time insure full freedom for the body turn.

When playing a tee shot, a fairway wood shot or a long iron shot I get a little something extra into it by the manner in which I utilize my right foot. Some say that I dig my right toe in when hitting a tee shot, but that description isn't correct because it isn't my toe I dig into the ground.

At address for the above-mentioned shots I dig in with the cleats on the inside edge of the sole of my right shoe. This gives me a feeling of solidity to hit from and as a result I get more distance by giving a little shove with my right foot as the club approaches the ball.

Yet I don't dig in so solidly that my foot is ever locked to the ground. Nor does my "digging in" interfere with the proper motion of the feet and the shifting of my weight during the swing. Maybe it will take you a little time to get onto the use of the little wrinkle I have described above, but it is the little variations which give me my extra power.

In the relationship between the stance and the arms the left arm is extended and the left elbow is not locked, but straight. Once the grip is assumed with the left hand the left arm automatically becomes part of the shaft.

The shaft of the club should be visualized as a rod from the point of the left shoulder to the clubhead with one hinge and that being the left wrist. In placing the right hand on the club make sure that the right arm is limp and that the right elbow is pointed down.

At the address there is no straightening of the right elbow. In order that the right arm will be limp and the right elbow down, one must list slightly from the right side. By list I mean that the right shoulder must be dropped and the hips faced slightly to the left.

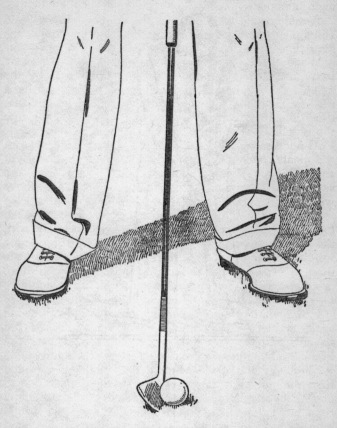

This picture shows the relation of the feet to one another. My weight is evenly distributed between both feet and the weight on each foot is from the ball of the foot back through the heel. The weight is never forward on your feet. My toes are pointed outward slightly.

The white tape in this and the next two pictures is used to illustrate the relationship of the feet to the line of flight in the various stances. In the square stance here my feet are square to the line of flight. A medium iron, a No. 5, is used in these pictures and the ball is played from a line which if extended back would run two inches inside of the left heel.

Open Stance. My left foot has been withdrawn from the line of flight as represented by the tape and my right foot has been advanced slightly beyond the line of flight. The ball remains constant in relation to the position of the feet. This stance encourages a fade or slice.

Closed Stance. My right foot has been withdrawn from the direction line and my left foot has been advanced slightly beyond the direction line. The position of the ball in relation to the feet is still constant. This stance encourages a draw or hook.

Open Stance, Rear View. This picture illustrates how much the position of the feet is altered to open the stance. My left foot is withdrawn from the line approximately one half inch while my right foot is advanced one half inch, making a change of approximately one inch.

Closed Stance, Rear View. My left foot is advanced approximately one half inch while my right foot has been withdrawn one half inch, making the overall alteration approximately one inch. These adjustments in the stance, slight as they may seem, are important. Reason: They alter the facing of the body.

Nine Iron Stance (Open Stance). As the number of the club decreases the stance gradually closes. The ball is played from a position on a line which if extended back would be approximately two inches inside the left heel. I have used a series of golf balls to show that this relationship between the ball and the feet is constant.

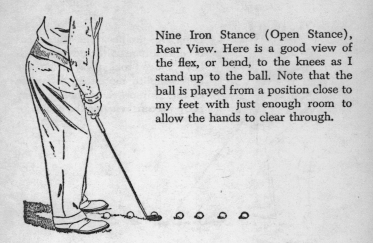

Nine Iron Stance (Open Stance),
Rear View. Here is a good view of
the flex, or bend, to the knees as I
stand up to the ball. Note that the
ball is played from a position close to
my feet with just enough room to
allow the hands to clear through.

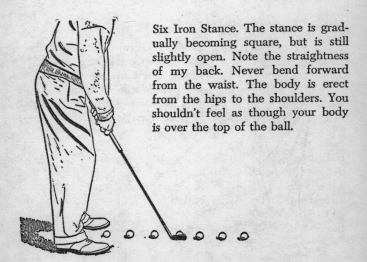

Six Iron Stance. The stance is gradually becoming square, but is still
slightly open. Note the straightness
of my back. Never bend forward
from the waist. The body is erect
from the hips to the shoulders. You
shouldn't feel as though your body
is over the top of the ball.

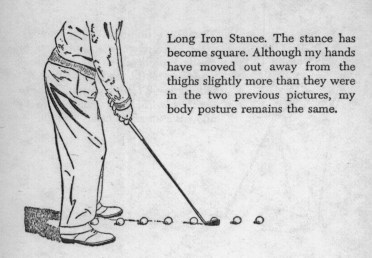

Long Iron Stance. The stance has become square. Although my hands have moved out away from the thighs slightly more than they were in the two previous pictures, my body posture remains the same.

Driver Stance. This is really a power stance, slightly closed. My hands and arms are about as far away from the body in this picture as they ever are, but the body posture remains the same.

Driver Stance, Front View. This picture clearly shows that the ball position is constant, being played from a line which if extended back would pass approximately two inches off the inside of the left heel. My stance has been widened by moving the right foot farther away from the left laterally as shown here. My feet are farther back away from the ball to accommodate the longer shaft and swing.

Here is a little trick which will enable you to check to see if your elbows are in the correct position when you take up your stance at the ball. I have inserted an iron club under the left elbow and over the inside of the right elbow to show that the right arm should be underneath the left.

CHAPTER IV

The Full Swing

THERE are two crises which the average golfer reaches during the course of the natural golf swing which might be called *The Crossroads of Golf*. Should you make a wrong turn at either of these crossroads there is nothing but disaster ahead.

The first of these comes at that moment when the clubhead moves away from the ball at the start of the backswing. The second occurs at the top of the backswing when it is time to start the downswing.

Discussing these crises in order, however, let us consider the first, which takes place at the exact moment when you move the clubhead away from the ball. The second of these crises will be discussed in the section of this chapter on the downswing because that is where it really belongs.

Naturally, to give you a better understanding of the full golf swing, I'll confine my remarks in this chapter to the full golf swing. I'm referring now to the type of golf swing used to play tee shots, fairway wood shots and long iron shots.

One of the questions I am most often asked is how the club is started back on the backswing. But most of the golfers who ask me that question don't even wait for my answer. Instead, they quickly offer the suggestion that maybe it is started back by the left hand, right hand, left arm or right arm. Usually they have one opinion or another, as outlined above, and want me to confirm their opinions. That is something I can't do.

Actually, the club is not started back in any of the ways they suggest. It starts back on the recoil from the forward press.

This forward press is nothing more than the movement forward of the hands, arms and body just before the backswing. What it amounts to is that you address the ball with some movement, or waggle as the tournament professionals call it, and then go smoothly from the waggle into the backswing via the recoil from the forward press.

The clubhead, the hands and the shoulders must all start back together in one motion. If you start them all back in one motion you are sure of a swing which will be well-timed throughout and with the major movements synchronized.

The club will be kept low going back, provided the player doesn't purposely pick it up with his hands. If allowed to pursue a normal course going back the club will describe an arc. Remember, however, that the club is definitely swung back just as it is swung down.

It is my firm belief that any golfer can achieve a certain amount of success by concentrating on the backswing. If it is not properly performed you can't expect much from the downswing which follows. Starting the backswing there is a definite turning motion of the hips.

A great deal has been said about how the club is started away from the ball—whether the clubface is square, opened or closed—but actually it neither opens nor closes during the backswing. It remains square throughout.

Going back on the backswing the shoulders and arms take a turning motion around the hub and this appears to open the face of the club, but actually it doesn't. The hands and wrists haven't rolled either over or under and for that reason the clubface remained square going back.

You can check this by taking up the position of address. Without moving your arms or body pick the club up by just breaking your wrists straight up. That's the only way that the wrists break at all during the swing. In that position the face of the club is still square to the line.

Now with your wrists broken move your hands back to the top of your swing and you will find that you are at the position you should be at the top of the swing. The clubface is still square.

The grip is firm throughout. However, there is more pressure on the last three fingers of the left hand than at any other place in your grip.

A quarter of the way back the wrists haven't cocked yet. In fact, there is no conscious cocking of the wrists at any time during the swing. The cocking of the wrists is gradual as you proceed with the backswing.

As the club goes back the left knee bends in toward the right knee. The left ankle is rolled in toward the right foot with the left heel coming off the ground only slightly. The weight is shifted back to the right leg with a very slight lateral movement of your hips.

The body only coils. Your head doesn't move. Visualize your neck as the hub of a wheel with your arms and shoulders rotating around this hub. This will insure a perfect arc of the club on both the backswing and the downswing.

The right leg does not straighten on the backswing. It should remain broken about the same amount as it was at the address.

The left arm is straight and the point of the left shoulder is underneath the chin and pointed down at the ball when the full backswing is completed.

At the top of your backswing the club should be held just as firmly in both hands as it was at the address. Any looseness in the grip can always cause you trouble, but particularly at this point because you are about to embark on the downswing.

Remember, however, a good downswing is dependent on your executing a good backswing. The backswing should be taken as one continuous rhythmic action. All movements are smooth and properly synchronized.

B—THE DOWNSWING

The downswing is said to start at the top of the swing, but that is not correct as there is no final top of the swing position. By the time the club reaches what is often referred to as the top of the swing, the downswing has really started. Exactly at that moment, however, you reach the second of the golfing crises, or crossroads, I outlined in my introductory paragraphs in this chapter.

The first movement in the downswing is the turning of the left hip to the left. Forget about your arms, hands, shoulders and club at that moment and start the hips turning, led by the left hip.

When the hips are turned to the left there will be enough lateral movement to put your weight on your left foot, unless, of course, there is a conscious effort to hold back weight on the right foot, which is wrong.

When you turn the left hip to start the downswing it gives the hands and arms a running start. In this way you create all the speed possible with your body before applying the arms and hands.

The turning of your hips brings your hands and club down toward the ball approximately three or four feet. You will then be in hitting position and ready for the hands, arms and club to come into play.

It is at this point in the swing, of course, where the hands, arms and club start to make a definite attempt to hit the ball, but not until then. In starting the club down with the turning of the hips you will be able to hit from the inside out. If the shoulders or hands initiated the movement from the top of the backswing you would be forced to hit from the outside in, which means trouble.

Right at this point is the second of the golfing crossroads, or crises, I have mentioned before. I believe that it is important to master the idea of starting the downswing with the turning of the hips because it is the difference between seventy and ninety plus golf.

While the hips are unwinding the weight is transferred to the left foot. Your shoulders should follow your hips around. If the hips follow the shoulders around you will find the club will travel from the outside in, which is wrong.

Just before the hands and arms come into play the body should be set for the hit. By that I mean that 90% of the weight should be on the left foot and the right arm should be very close to the body.

All tension should be released from the right leg and hip. The right knee should break in toward the left knee. The wrists uncock, the right arm straightens and then turns over in going forward over the left shoulder. This all takes place in that sequence and you will find that it will bring you to the complete finish.

If you have started the downswing correctly you have to hit from the inside out because the clubhead will always be approaching the ball from the inside.

The inside-out phase of the swing is important at all times during the swing, but particularly when you are playing irons.

The next time you get a chance to see a good player in action take note of how his body appears to drive forward before he hits the ball. This causes the club to travel inside of the arc it described going back on the backswing.

The most common faults of the inexperienced player during the downswing are hurrying into the downswing before the backswing is completed, rushing the right shoulder around before the clubhead reaches the hitting area and turning the upper part of the body into the shot too quickly. These errors throw your timing off and without proper timing you can't hope to attain the maximum distance.

The application of speed and power to the golf swing is not a hurry-up process. Speed and power are gradually applied during the golf swing and increased until they reach their climax right on the ball. The distance the ball travels when hit is determined by the speed of the clubhead at impact.

Tests have revealed that the top golfers attain their maximum hand action speed at the moment of impact, whereas the duffer is losing it as his club approaches the ball. Usually this is the result of trying to hurry either the backswing, the downswing or both by hitting from the top.

By means of magnificent control the top golfers cut loose with their maximum hand action speed just before the moment of impact. During the downswing the arms are kept in close to the body and the right shoulder goes underneath. The wrists are uncocked and straightened out at the last possible moment before impact, generating tremendous power.

The transfer of the weight back to the left leg is almost an automatic reaction, provided the hip action is correct. The head and shoulders stay behind the swing. The head remains in its original position throughout the swing, the head and neck serving as the hub of the swing.

Of course, the hands are moving at top speed, but right here one of the most common errors is a forward bend of the wrists which will result in the clubhead being ahead of the hands. Instead the wrists are straightened out as I have described above and the player should really be turning loose everything he has.

The finish of the swing should cause you no great concern. It merely serves to indicate how well you have carried out the fundamentals of the swing.

When all motion of the full swing has ceased your head should be turned to face the line of flight. Your eyes should be on the flight of the ball. The body has also turned toward the line of flight and most of the weight has shifted over onto the left leg.

After a lot of practice, all of the movements I have described should become muscle-memory and will require no great amount of thought on your part to execute them perfectly. You can then concentrate on hitting the ball and the golfing problem confronting you and really capitalize on the power such a swing generates.

Address. My feet are as far apart as width of shoulders. Toes
are out, weight back through the feet, knees flexed and bent
in toward each other. Right arm is relaxed and lower than
left. Left elbow is pointing toward the left hip and right elbow
toward the right hip. This shot calls for a full application of
power, but note absence of any appearance of strain.

Starting the club back, the hips, shoulders, arms and hands
move simultaneously. This takes the club low along the ground
and insures you a full arc.

My wrists start to break about the waist line. My left knee has begun to break inward toward the right, the weight is shifting to the right foot.

My left ankle starts to roll in toward the right foot. The left knee has broken in toward the right knee. Note that the right knee is still flexed the same amount as it was at the address. Hips and shoulders are still coiling.

My wrists are almost broken to their maximum. The right elbow points down. The left arm is straight. The left shoulder turns underneath the chin.

At top of swing my left ankle has rolled to its maximum and the left knee has bent in toward the right knee to its maximum. About 85% of my weight is on the right foot and leg. Right knee is flexed the same and right leg is at the same angle as at address. Hips and shoulders have turned to their maximum. Head is still in same position as at address while the left arm remains straight.

Hips turn to the left to start downswing. Forget about the shoulders, arms and hands. The downswing is initiated by the turning of the left hip.

My hips have turned back halfway and the shoulders have turned one quarter. In that order these two movements have moved the hands down approximately two feet nearer the position at the ball.

My hips and shoulders are still turning to the left in that order. They are still pulling the arms and hands down and around into position for their work. Note that the wrists are still fully cocked. My right knee has begun to bend in toward the left knee. The body is producing power.

At this point my body has produced all of the power it possibly can on the downswing and now the arms and hands are starting to generate their power. The wrists are just beginning to uncock and the right foot is giving that decided push I use to get added power.

My body is set for the hit and 85% of the weight is now on the left foot. My right elbow is tucked into the right side. The push with the right foot mentioned in the previous picture caption is even more evident.

The head is still stationary, the right elbow is almost ready to straighten while the wrists have almost fully uncocked. My left knee is flexed the same amount as at address. Note the impression of power here.

Wrists are fully uncocked. Right arm is straightening. Now 95% of the weight is transferred to the left foot. The right knee has broken in toward the left knee to a maximum degree and the right side of the body is completely relaxed. My left knee is still flexed, it has not straightened.

The hips and shoulders are still turning. My right shoulder is now moving underneath the chin. There is a full extension of the arms and hands.

My hands are now pronating, or turning over, the left arm
is beginning to break and the right arm is fully extended with
the shoulders and hips turned to their maximum as I follow
through on the swing.

The speed and momentum of the club has carried me to a full finish.

CHAPTER V

Turning On the Power

THE golfers of today are distance-minded, even the week-end golfers. I know that to be true because so many of them come to me during the course of my travels around the country and want to know how they can get more distance.

They have the strength and the golfing ability, but they don't know how to make the most of what they have. No matter how big and strong you are it doesn't mean a thing in golf, unless you know how to apply your strength. Distance is obtained by a full use of your physical faculties and strength in combination with perfect timing.

My advice to the beginning golfer is to go ahead and hit the ball as hard as he can right from the start. He will be wild for a time. That's only natural. Later on he can straighten out his hooks and slices with minor alterations to his swing. But if he doesn't learn to hit the ball hard right at the start, he will never be able to get distance without a major overhauling, because his speed and timing setup will be for something less than his full power.

The tournament golfers of today are shooting for birdies all of the time. Within reason, we try to hit our tee shots as far as we possibly can. Naturally, we don't hit them as hard as we can if there is a chance that they will land in a group of trees or some other hazard.

Moreover, the location of the pin on the greens doesn't

discourage us in our quest for birdies. No matter where they put the pins we shoot for them and try to get down in as few strokes as possible.

Before I go into detail on how I turn on the power, let me say that I don't go out and blaze away with all of my power on every hole. I pick my spots.

The long par fours or the long par fives are the holes I usually select to cut loose on with all of my extra power in an effort to get birdies. The idea behind the turning on of your extra power on these holes is to get as far out off the tee as possible in the hope that you won't have a wood shot to the green for your second shot.

Most par five holes offer you an excellent chance to score in sub-par figures if you can get any distance at all off the tee. Pump the ball out as far as you can and reach the green in two on these holes if it is at all humanly possible for you to get there.

In reviewing the changes in the game that have given us tournament golfers increased and controlled power, let's start with the grip and stance. We now grip our clubs more firmly than they have ever been gripped. By using a firmer grip we are able to hit with greater authority and at the same time maintain complete control of the clubhead.

As for the stance, it is now considerably wider than it ever was. The purpose of the widened stance is to create greater traction with the feet. This widened stance and increased traction anchors us so that we are able to apply additional power to the swing through the legs while still maintaining perfect balance.

We also create additional power by first applying all of the body that we can to the swing. More power can be efficiently applied on the downswing by having the hips turn to the left, the shoulders follow, and then the arms and hands contribute their power.

Body action plays an important part in the golf swing when the body turns as fast as possible from the top of the swing to the left. Don't stop your body once you have initiated the swing. Keep it moving throughout if you want to develop power.

Of course, all of the above applies chiefly to wood shots, but additional power and distance can also be gained on iron shots in the same manner.

Gene Sarazen, who really spans two generations of golf, summed up the importance of the changes in the game I have outlined above after I had congratulated him on the way he played in a recent tournament in which we happened to be paired together.

"If I had driven as well in my day as I do now," said Sarazen, after thanking me for my congratulations, "I would have won more tournaments than I did.

"In my prime I was extremely wild off the tee. As a result I had to work much harder to score than I do now."

The reason that Gene's scores don't indicate his improvement is that he isn't as keen competitively as he used to be. If he were, he would still be winning tournaments.

WOOD SHOTS FOR DISTANCE

Golf, to my way of thinking, is broken down into three departments, woods, irons and putts. And each department is equally as important. If there is one department that is more important than the others, however, it would probably be the wood shots.

Suppose I tell a little story here to prove my point, comparing golf to the game of billiards. In billiards the player must control his cue ball at all times to set up his next shot. It's the same in golf: the player must control his tee shots in order to set up his next shot.

If the wood shots go astray you could be the best iron player in the world, but you would have no real chance to prove it because you would be playing from out of the rough and bunkers or from behind trees all of the time. Whereas if your tee shots are controlled your iron play problems will be much simpler. Which means, in turn, that your short game and putting problems are also simplified because you can always be on the offense instead of the defense.

When controlled, a tee shot sets up the second shot and

simplifies it. Since the second shot is simplified, it stands to reason that the third shot, which normally is the putt, will be relatively easy.

"What are the chief differences between the swing you use for wood shots and the swing you use for iron shots?" is a question quite frequently asked of golf instructors. The answer, as far as I am concerned, is that there should be no great conscious difference in the swings used. Once you've grooved your swing you shouldn't be conscious of making any fundamental changes no matter what club you are using.

Strictly speaking, of course, there are differences in the swings, but they should be so slight as to be relatively unimportant to the over-all idea of the swing. Very few golfers actually swing exactly alike, but there are any number who follow the same fundamentals in playing the game.

Naturally with a wood club the action of the swing is slower because the swing is longer. With an iron the action of the swing is speeded up, but fundamentally it is the same swing. When you use your wood clubs you are trying to hit the ball as far as you can, whereas when you use an iron you are trying to combine distance and accuracy so efficiently that the ball will drop into the cup.

When you are shooting at a green with a wood club you must remember that you have a much smaller target because it is very difficult to hit the green with a wood club and hold the ball on it. That's because the ball comes onto the green off the wood club very fast and with very little bite, or backspin, on it.

At the same time, however, don't underestimate the value of learning how to control your wood shots. The errors you make on the tee probably won't impress you as to just how much they have cost you in strokes as much as errors you have committed much closer to the green. But break down your scores and you will find your tee shot errors are costly enough.

For instance, I covered my own experiences while seeking a new driver to fit my game in the chapter *Clubs*

. . . Selection and Use. However, the value of having a
driver which fits your game and thus enables you to
control your tee shots was never more powerfully illus-
trated than in the playoff between Lew Worsham and
Sam Snead for the 1947 United States Open Golf Championship at St. Louis, won by Worsham, so let's discuss
that match. Snead, like yours truly, elected to use a
brassie off the tee in the Open because he had been
having trouble with his drives in the tournaments prior
to that event. Sam drove beautifully with that club during the course of the regular matches, but the gamble he
made when he drove with a brassie in lieu of a driver
caught up with him in the playoff.

The brassie has more loft than a driver. It gives you
more height which means that if the wind happens to be
blowing at all you are more at its mercy than you would
be with a driver.

During the Snead-Worsham playoff it seemed that
every time Snead assumed a commanding margin his tee
shots betrayed him. For instance, stepping onto the sixth
tee he had a two stroke lead on Worsham, but drove into
the rough. By the time he got the ball into the cup at that
hole he was over par for it and had lost his margin of
lead. Again at the tenth, eleventh, thirteenth, fifteenth
and seventeenth, Snead's tee shots strayed off line. That
is a lot of tee shot errors to make in a match for the U.S.
Open Championship and I have to think that they cost
Sam the title.

Sam's miscue at the fifteenth tee was particularly
disastrous. Going to that hole Sam had a one stroke lead,
but after he drove into the rough he bogeyed the hole
and lost his advantage. Snead and Worsham were all
even at the eighteenth and Lew won the title, by one
shot, when he went into the lead for the first time during
the match.

While Worsham is a long hitter off the tee, getting
plenty of roll on his ball after it lands on the fairways, I
am not sure that he would be able to consistently outdrive
Snead the way he did during that playoff if Sam had
been able to find a driver to fit his game in time for that

event. The golfing moral of this, of course, is to be sure you pick a driver to fit you when selecting your clubs and to keep working to retain your sharpness with this club.

Concentrate on combining accuracy and consistency with distance when playing your wood clubs. Starting with the grip, I play my wood clubs with *The Full Swing* I have outlined in the chapter of that title on that department of my game. The stance I favor for my wood clubs, and, in fact, for all my long clubs from the three iron right on up through the driver, however, is a slightly closed stance because it provides more traction and better balance.

This stance enables you to strike the more powerful blow required to get the most out of these clubs. In order to get real distance with them you have to be firmly anchored. Another reason why I favor this stance on these shots is that it enables you to turn your body more freely and freedom of body turn permits you to lengthen the arc of your swing for the longer shots.

Remember when taking up this stance to turn both toes out slightly. It will aid you to keep your balance during the full swing and at the same time permit you freedom of the body and legs for the body turn used to get a little something extra into distance shots.

When playing a tee shot, a fairway wood shot or any long iron shot that I can afford to cut loose on, I get a little something extra into it by the manner in which I utilize my right foot. (Described in the chapter *Stance Gives You Balance.*) During the course of my swing I dig in with the cleats on the inside edge of the sole of my right shoe. During the course of the downswing, and just before impact, a decided push is given with this foot which helps to speed up the club.

Naturally, it will come in mighty handy if you are able to slice and hook at will with a wood club and still retain control of the ball. These are variations, however, which require a little more finesse and a little more knowledge of the mechanics of the golf swing than the average duffer has acquired.

One of the first steps you can take toward learning how to play variation shots with your wood clubs is to learn to control the flight of the ball, high or low, at will. This will come in mighty handy when there is a strong wind blowing because a high shot in a strong wind is absolutely at the mercy of the wind and can be extremely costly when you total up your strokes.

When the wind is blowing a low shot, or quail high as we say in Texas, will bite right into the wind and cover more distance than you would ordinarily get under the same conditions with a normal flight of the ball. The technique on how to play this shot is discussed in the chapter *Stormy Weather Golf* in the section on wind shots.

Fundamentally, the brassie is the longest club off the fairway, but you will probably get better results, in most instances, with a No. 3 wood. Tournament professionals generally use the No. 3 wood. They seldom take a brassie unless it is in desperation.

If you are playing a course with wonderful fairways, where the ball always sits up, and a maximum of distance is required, the brassie is the club to use. I would also qualify its use further, however, by stating that even in such circumstances you should be very proficient with a straight-faced club before you resort to the brassie.

Using the No. 3 and No. 4 Woods

Before you attempt to use the No. 3 and No. 4 wood clubs you should have a good idea of where and when to use each to an advantage. For instance, I use my No. 3 wood club as a general utility club off the fairways. Wherever the shot calls for length and accuracy I take my trusty No. 3 out of the bag. However, when I have to gamble, the No. 4 wood is my selection.

I also take my No. 4 wood when length is required and the ball is in a lie that is not too good. When the bunker in front of me is not too high and distance is required, I gamble by taking my No. 4 wood to play a shot out of a trap. By the way, when using the No. 4 wood out of a bunker be sure you hit the ball, not the sand behind it. It is amazing what distance you will get out of the rough with the No. 4 wood.

The reason you get distance out of the rough with the No. 4 wood is that, like all wood clubs, it has a knoblike head and doesn't cut the grass like an iron club, but spreads it. When you cut the grass, as you can't help doing with an iron club because of its blade, some of the club action speed is lost. This doesn't happen with the wood club. Another reason why the No. 4 wood is so effective when used to get the ball up out of the grass is because it has so much loft on the clubface. It might surprise you to know, for instance, that the No. 4 wood has more loft than a No. 3 iron.

Address. Weight is evenly distributed between both feet. The stance is closed slightly, the toes out, knees flexed, the body almost straight from the hips to the shoulders and the arms are hanging down fully extended. There is no strain in this setup, no feeling of reaching for the ball.

The club is being started back by the winding up of my hips, shoulders, arms and hands and with no attempt being made to break the wrists.

My body is still winding up. There is a full extension of arms and hands. The head remains stationary through backswing and downswing.

The wrists have begun to break. My left knee is breaking in toward the right knee while the right knee is still flexed. The right knee has not straightened, nor does it ever straighten on the backswing.

The left shoulder is now moving underneath the chin, the left arm is straight and the right arm has almost completed the maximum bend. Take note that my right elbow is pointing down, not out.

At the top of the backswing a line extended from the end of my grip through my left arm would extend straight to the ball. This means that my swing is neither too upright nor too flat. If this line would extend beyond the ball my swing would be too flat. If extended short of the ball my swing would be too upright. My right knee is still flexed as at address and my left heel has come off the ground only slightly.

My hips are still leading the shoulder turn. Both arms and hands are still in the same relative positions they were at the top of the swing. Power and speed have been obtained by just the turning of the hips.

My body did its work on the downswing by pulling the arms
and hands into position, plus initiating the swing from the
top and creating all the early speed. Arms and hands are now
ready to do their job.

My wrists are uncocking at the proper place, accelerating the club just before impact. Notice that the right leg is completely relaxed at this point.

Even as the ball is being struck my hips have continued to turn. The left hip has been moved to the left and out of the way to allow room enough for the arms and hands to pass at their maximum speed. My right and left arms are still in the same relationship as they were at address.

My right arm has now straightened to its maximum and both arms are fully extended. My right shoulder is turning underneath the chin.

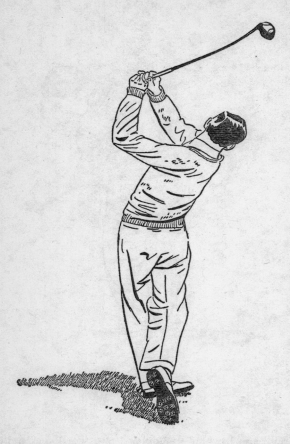

The left arm has broken almost to its maximum and my left elbow is pointing down and not out. The right arm is still fully extended. This is just the reverse of the backswing. On the backswing the left arm was straight and the right arm was broken with the right elbow pointing down.

The finish of the swing. The wrists have completed their pronation, or turning, the left arm is broken to its maximum
with the left elbow pointing down. Notice that on the finish
95% of the weight is on the outside of the left foot. The right
side is completely relaxed.

This sequence of pictures emphasizes how important it is to initiate the body action at the top of the swing to hit a longer ball. The left arm is straight, the chin is on the point of the left shoulder, the knees flexed and the weight shifted so that the outside of the left foot is off the ground. I am not cramped. Fluidity is evident in this picture. Before the body initiates this downward swing and produces speed the right knee must remain flexed as at address, not locked.

My left hip is turning to the left. There is enough lateral
movement to shift my weight from the right foot to the left.
Let your shoulders, arms and hands lag back and let the
tension in your back and side muscles bring the shoulders,
arms and hands around with the turn of the hips.

The left hip has turned in advance of the left shoulder. My arms are still in the same relative position as they were at the top of the swing. Wrists are still fully cocked, although the hands are almost at the waistline.

Set for the hit. My hips are still turning. The shoulders haven't caught up with my hips and they won't until the finish. My wrists are just now uncocking, although my left hand has almost pulled even with the ball. The right knee is bent inward and it is quite evident that the right foot is giving the little shove I told you about in the text.

CHAPTER VI

Iron Shots for Accuracy

PRIDE will inspire most golfers to do a certain amount of practice work on their tee shots and their putting, but the same gents will let their iron play deteriorate without giving it a thought. Yet iron play is every bit as important to them as an ability to hit a tee shot straight and to putt accurately because iron shots are the accuracy shots of golf.

By that I don't mean to imply that you don't have to be accurate with your wood clubs. You do. The difference lies in the fact that the margin of error for iron shots is less than for your wood clubs.

Iron shots are also the offensive shots of golf. That's because it is impossible to score a course consistently well without hitting good iron shots. I say that in spite of the fact that I have seen many low scores posted without the aid of good iron play.

Whenever that has happened, however, it has invariably been done the hard way by means of phenomenal putting. Maybe you can offset your errors in iron play technique with good putting for an occasional round or two, but never over a period of time. Ability with a putter is a great asset, but it can't compensate for faulty iron play indefinitely.

Good golfers attack a golf course right from the first tee shot in order to put themselves in command of the situation as soon as possible. On the other hand a faulty iron player must immediately go on the defensive, avoid as many errors as he can and rely on his short game for any help at all in cutting down his score.

Hitting a good iron shot is more difficult than hitting a good wood shot. The reason for this is the ball must be contacted properly with the blade of the club and the blow struck with a sharpness of impact that is never experienced with a wood club.

If there is any great difference between an iron shot and a wood shot it is that an iron shot is definitely a sharp hit while a wood shot is swung and the ball swept off either the tee or the turf. Since the iron swing is shorter than that used in playing a wood shot, because the length of the shaft of an iron club is shorter than that on a wood and because the ball must be contacted on the downswing, the action of the body and the hands must be speeded up considerably.

Summing up the approach to iron play, let me say that the only variations you will have to concern yourself with are the stance and the length of the swing.

Naturally, while you are playing the various iron clubs your stance varies. A good key to the amount of this variation is to remember that as the numbers of your irons increase the width of your stance decreases and also opens. Stances won't be discussed here in relation to iron play, however, because all of the stances are discussed at length in the chapter *Stance Gives You Balance*.

When you are using an iron club the swing automatically becomes more upright because of the length of the club shaft. The length of the swing is graduated. For instance, you take a longer swing with a one iron than you do with a nine iron.

While playing iron shots you have to be extremely careful in judging the distance and straightness of the shot required. You must also remember that you have a maximum, medium and minimum range with each iron from the four iron down to the nine iron, particularly from the six iron down, and play each shot accordingly.

The reason it is important for you to realize the

limitations of your irons is that if you took your irons back on the backswing as you do the driver, for instance, you would have too much sway. In iron play the wrists are broken much sooner on the backswing than they are when you are playing wood shots. This enables you to hit down and through the ball.

To accomplish this the weight is shifted to the left side faster on an iron shot than it is when you use a wood club. This brings the lowest part of the swing in front of the ball, enabling you to hit down on the ball and take turf in front of it, not in back.

Let me digress here a moment to say that a question I am asked quite frequently is, "Why do novice golfers take turf in back of the ball on iron shots instead of in front of it as the professionals do?"

Of course, it is difficult to answer that question accurately and completely without having a chance to study the individuals involved, but generally the novice golfer takes turf in back of the ball because he has started with most of his weight on the right foot at address and on the backswing shifts the remainder of his weight to the right foot and on the downswing fails to shift his weight over to his left foot. As a result he will continually hit in back of the ball and take turf there instead of in front of it.

Shift your weight to the left foot at the top of the swing as you would when using your driver. But be sure to make a conscious effort to do it much sooner and faster than you do when using the wood clubs. This shifting of the weight rapidly brings the lowest part of the swing in front of the ball. You are thus sure of hitting down on the ball. And when you do that you will take turf in front of it and not in back of it.

Just as with the wood clubs the clubhead, hands and shoulders must all start back in one motion. Going back there is a very slight lateral movement of the hips. Remember that the backswing is one continuous rhythmic motion.

The first movement in the downswing for the long irons is, likewise just as it was with the woods, the turning of the left hip to the left. When the hips are turned to the left there is enough lateral movement to put your weight on your left foot.

Hitting down is an important part of iron play. With the exception of the putter and the driver remember that you hit down on every other shot in golf.

The reason hitting down is so important on iron shots is that it is the only way that you can hit the ball squarely while still imparting a degree of underspin to it. You have to have a greater degree of underspin on iron shots than you have on any other shots because this underspin is absolutely necessary for control and control is more important on iron shots than anything else.

Mention of underspin recalls to mind the fact that much has been written and said about hitting a golf ball with overspin. It has been the subject of discussion for some time, but I contend that there is no such thing as overspin on any shot with the possible exception of one that is topped.

The reason I contend that there is no such thing as overspin is that in order to get any ball up into the air you have to impart underspin to it. Otherwise it wouldn't go up.

On occasion you will see a ball hit the green and run for a considerable distance. Perhaps you have been under the impression that such a ball has overspin on it. Take it from me, it hasn't.

Actually, it has what can be best described as a minimum of underspin. You can hit a golf ball with a maximum of underspin and a minimum of underspin and several variations somewhere in between the two. Underspin is also sometimes referred to as backspin.

Whether you use a minimum of underspin or a maximum should depend on the situation you are confronted with. For instance, a minimum of underspin is called for on a tee shot. The farther the ball goes the better most of us like it on tee shots, particularly if the tee shot is straight and we manage to keep out of trouble. On the other hand, on shots to the green a maximum of underspin, or backspin, is required or the ball wouldn't hold the green.

A maximum of underspin must be imparted to the ball for extreme efficiency on most iron shots. Without a maximum of underspin an iron shot can't be controlled as to length, direction or height. Underspin is imparted by having the blade of the club contact the ball first in a downward motion and, of course, taking turf afterwards as the blow is continued on down.

There must also be a sharpness to the blow struck. By that I mean that the ball must be hit hard with the hands during the course of the swing. Hit the ball as if you were driving it forward, letting the loft of the club blade itself provide the necessary height to the flight of the ball.

There are times, of course, when a soft shot is required. This is accomplished by slowing down, especially the hand action and the body movement for a lob shot. This type of shot is only used on short shots around the green when the ball must rise quickly.

Sometimes in hitting to the green you will find yourself in a situation where it is impossible to impart the maximum of underspin to the ball and still get enough distance to reach the green. You are not able to hold the ball on the green even if you reach it because you have sacrificed underspin for distance.

The club in your bag which will impart the most underspin, or backspin, to the ball is the five iron. I don't know why that should be true, but it has been tested and proved to be a fact.

Of course, you don't hit as hard with a nine iron as you do, for instance, with a five iron. Considering the amount of loft you have, the amount of power you use, and the flight of the ball you get, however, the five iron is the club which gives you the most underspin and, therefore, provides you with the most control of the ball.

The one iron, or driving iron, is the most difficult club in the bag to master. In order to obtain maximum results with it you have to use more power than with any other club.

There is so little loft on a one iron that you have the double problem of trying to hit this shot much harder while still trying to get the ball into the air with a controlled flight. This means that in order to accomplish that, you must reach the lowest arc of your swing just in front of the ball.

The reason this is essential is that it is the only way that you can hit the ball squarely and at the same time impart the degree of underspin which is absolutely necessary for control. Again I emphasize the fact that you must have a great degree of underspin on iron shots to maintain any control of them at all.

The reason why most players of the English school of golf, and I will include Bobby Locke in that school, don't control their shots to the green as well as the American professionals do is that they don't use the underspin mentioned here. We drive the ball into the greens with a lower trajectory, more authority and more control, whereas the players of the English school prefer to lob it to the greens.

I've also been told by English players who have visited here that we practice our iron shots more than they do. This constant practice enables us to keep our iron shots crisp while still maintaining control of them.

PITCH AND CHIP SHOTS

Two different iron shots which are almost always sure to confuse the beginning golfer are chip shots and pitch shots. Perhaps it will simplify matters if I say that when the ball is twenty yards, or less, from the green I play a chip shot. When it is more than twenty yards from the green I play a pitch shot.

The chief difference between these two shots, in relation to the use of the body at least, is that where a pitch shot calls for a moderate amount of body movement, a chip shot requires no movement of the body worth mentioning.

There is also a difference in the clubs selected to make this shot. Never take more than a four iron to make a chip shot. The one, two and three irons are not practical because they haven't enough loft. The reason for taking a club with more loft than that provided by the one, two or three iron is that the chip shot must be hit so easily that it is impossible to get the ball up off the ground with any flight at all with one of the lesser lofted clubs.

In fact, the most common error in attempting a chip shot is not taking a club with enough loft. For example, I very seldom take less loft than a six iron for this shot.

Whatever you do, don't make the mistake of chipping the ball so that it rolls most of the way. Figure on a certain amount of roll, but not too much. For instance, with a seven iron chip the ball about 15 feet and figure on another 15 feet of roll.

When chipping I try to place the ball where I will get an uphill putt. I don't want a downhill putt, if I can help it, because if I miss it I am apt to have another putt of about the same distance coming back. So I check the green carefully before making a chip shot.

The ball is played very close to your feet. Once again assume the tripod posture I have mentioned before.

The club is taken back with the hands only. The right elbow rests on the right hip to insure the arms, hands and club a pivotal point. If you set up this pivotal point correctly you reduce the margin of error and your club will return to the place from which you addressed the ball.

On the address remember to open the stance considerably on chip shots and use about a quarter turn of your body. The weight has to be on the left foot on this shot because it brings the lowest part of the swing in front of the ball, enabling you to hit the ball first and then take turf with the blade of the club. If the weight is equally distributed between the two feet or on the right foot you will find yourself hitting behind the ball or half topping it.

Let the loft of the club pick the ball up. Never try to loft the ball with some movement of your body or hands. If you need more loft get a loftier club, but don't try to swing under the ball.

Make sure that both hands ride along with the shaft

of the club. Don't let the head of the club come up. Keep the head of the club as low to the ground as possible at the finish.

Starting at the address the hands should be well forward and should be kept there. Try to get your hands out in front of the clubhead and keep them there during the swing.

There are all kinds of pitch shots. Some players loft the ball up, others play the ball low with a lot of bite on it. Bobby Locke, the South African, plays this shot with more loft on the ball than the American players. We prefer to play the shot low and with a lot of bite on the ball.

In making a lob shot to the green be sure to take a club with plenty of loft. The clubface is open, the ball more forward in relation to the feet than is usually customary. The swing is slow, the ball is not hit hard and very little turf is taken.

The low pitch shot with a bite on the ball might be played with the same club as the lob shot, but the position of the ball in relation to the feet is different. It is back more toward the right foot.

Your hands are in front of the clubhead and the wrists are broken rapidly on the backswing. The swing is short, but brought down into the ball so that it is hit hard. As you hit the ball the hands continue to remain in front of the clubhead. The weight is well forward on the left foot.

Mention of the pitch shots recalls to mind that quite often the novice doesn't realize that this shot can be made with a sand wedge. The heavy sand wedge used by the professionals and described in detail in the chapter on bunker shots is ideal for pitch shots.

Probably one reason why most novice golfers don't use the sand wedge on pitch shots is that they hesitate to make pitch shots.

The sand wedge is ideal for these shots because the blade has plenty of loft and the flange prevents the club blade from digging into the turf. If you gauge the shot correctly the ball should fly right up on the green.

Experiment with this club a little to find out what your maximum distance with it is. Then go ahead and start using it for all pitch shots from your maximum distance right on in to the green.

You can also use the eight iron and nine iron to play pitch shots to the green. For that reason they are very important clubs to the player working to reduce his score.

On this shot the ball must be hit downward. That is necessary in order for you to get underspin, or backspin, on the ball and thus control it. Provided you get the proper amount of backspin on the ball, this shot will make the ball stop soon after it lands on the green.

Watch the tournament golfers play the pitch shot and you will notice that they will rely on the loft of the clubface to provide the right amount of height to the ball. They make no effort to scoop or lift the ball into the air by means of false hand action.

In stepping up to the ball to make this shot, the feet are fairly close together. The stance is slightly open, the right foot being slightly nearer the intended line of flight.

As in all golf shots, the action is unhurried at the beginning of the downswing. There is a moderate amount of body movement. The feature of this shot, however, is the very definite amount of hand action at impact. In fact, both the hands and arms are very active in this shot, but it definitely is not made with a scooping motion.

Another thing to remember in using the eight iron and nine iron is that the clubhead travels through the ball following along the intended line of flight.

VARIATIONS

Quite often during the course of a round of golf you are faced with the problem of getting around obstacles such as trees, stones, and buildings. To accomplish it you will have to play either a slice or a hook as the case may be. On a slice the ball will turn to the right in flight, while on a hook it will curve to the left.

Many golfers are plagued with a slice or a hook while

trying to make a straight shot, but you're not a finished golfer until you control slices and hooks to your own advantage on the golf course. The grips for these variation shots are described and discussed in the chapter *Evolution of the Hogan Grip* while the stances for them will be found in the chapter *Stance Gives You Balance.*

For the slice play the ball from a normal position. However, your clubface and stance are opened considerably. Do not pronate the hands or roll the wrists. Make sure that the clubface remains open. Aim to the left, making an allowance for the curve you have to make around the obstacle in question.

Hooked iron shots are just the reverse. The stance is closed. Aim to the right. Turn the face of the club in at address.

On the hook as the club comes into the ball on the downswing the hands are now rolled over, or pronated, to the left. On both the hook and the slice the ball should be hit on the downswing and turf should be taken after the ball is struck.

The curved flight of the ball on both the hook and the slice is caused by the spin imparted as the clubhead cuts across the ball at any angle. These two shots, the slice and the hook, will be very valuable to you not only for their positive value in getting around obstacles, but in a negative sense as well because in order to learn to play an intentional slice or an intentional hook you must have a full knowledge of these shots. Many golfers have a permanent slice or a permanent hook, but these shots are only of value when you have full control of them.

Whatever kind of iron you choose to play each shot is a study. Take the time to select the proper club and shot required. Consider the trajectory required, the distance the ball must travel and the lie. However, if the lie does not permit the required shot, sacrifice either height or distance or both and play for a spot which will leave you a simple shot as your next one. Take particular pains to select the correct club because a straight shot either too long or too short is just as costly as one off line.

In addressing the chip shot remember to open the stance considerably. My feet are close together with the left toe pointed out. The knees are flexed. The hips are facing the hole about a quarter turn. The back is fairly straight, bend over only with the neck.

The ball is close to the feet. Never reach on this shot. The arms and hands are close in to the body. The club is taken back with the hands only. Right elbow rests on right hip, insuring the arms, hands and club a pivotal point. If you set this pivotal point up correctly you reduce the margin of error on this shot.

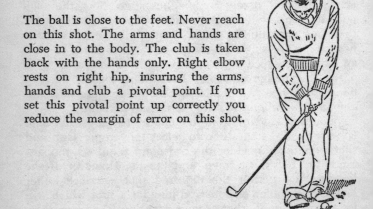

Let the loft of the club pick the ball up. Don't try to swing under it. On the downswing try not to let the clubhead get ahead of the hands. If anything, try to keep the hands in front of the club.

On the follow-through of a chip shot the clubhead remains low to the ground. There is no conscious effort of trying to pick the ball up with your hands. Make the swing smooth and unhurried.

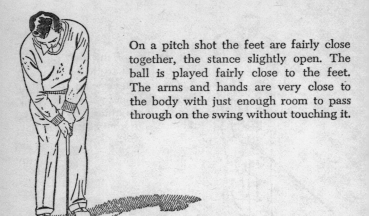

On a pitch shot the feet are fairly close together, the stance slightly open. The ball is played fairly close to the feet. The arms and hands are very close to the body with just enough room to pass through on the swing without touching it.

The wrists are broken rapidly on the backswing. The hands and left arm actually initiate it.

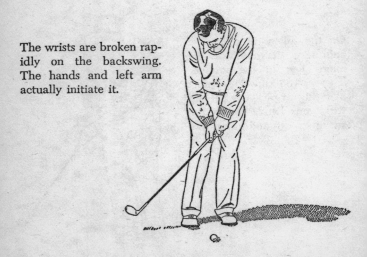

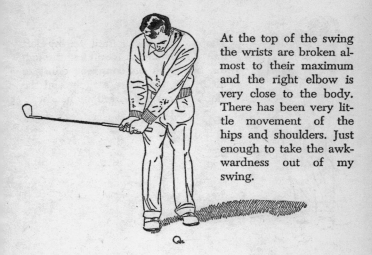

At the top of the swing the wrists are broken almost to their maximum and the right elbow is very close to the body. There has been very little movement of the hips and shoulders. Just enough to take the awkwardness out of my swing.

Starting the club down and through the ball, the downswing is initiated by turning the left hip. The wrists only uncock at impact. The hands are forward of the clubhead at impact.

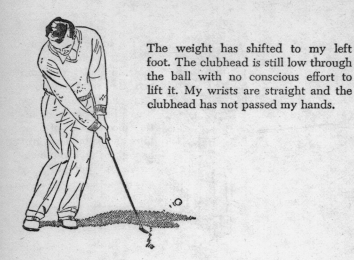

The weight has shifted to my left foot. The clubhead is still low through the ball with no conscious effort to lift it. My wrists are straight and the clubhead has not passed my hands.

Note that my right side has relaxed, the weight is on the outside of my left foot. This picture also shows that there has been a moderate amount of body movement, that this swing has been smooth and unhurried. The hands have not pronated and they never do on this shot.

At address for a short iron shot the stance is a little open, the left foot withdrawn slightly from the direction line. As the distance range of the club increases the right foot is moved laterally away from the left. On a chip shot the feet are almost together, on a pitch shot they're a little wider apart and on a short iron shot they're still wider apart.

Starting the backswing, once again the shoulders, arms, hands and hips start back simultaneously in one rhythmic movement.

For the short irons the wrists break just before reaching the waistline.

At the top of the swing the wrists are broken to their maximum as they are on all other shots with the exception of a chip shot. All the body movements in the short iron shots are somewhat minimized on the backswing.

Starting down the action immediately becomes sharper and faster to move your weight to the left side in order that the club will hit the ball on the downswing, which is your objective on iron shots.

The weight is being shifted over hurriedly to the left side.

Note the sharp acceleration of my body action and that this shot is primarily made with a downward blow. My wrists are not entirely uncocked as yet in spite of the fact that my left hand is almost past the ball.

Here the picture shows my club at the moment of impact. Close examination will show you that my hands are slightly in advance of the clubhead. Bang right into the ball. Don't try to pick it off.

Even after the ball has left the club the hands are still in advance of the clubhead. The loft of the club has picked the ball up. No attempt has been made to pick it up with some faulty movement of the hands.

My right leg is completely relaxed. My arms and hands are
fully extended.

In this picture my right arm is fully extended. My left arm has begun to break and the wrists are completing their pronation, or turning.

With the medium iron my stance has now become square. Again the modified sitting position is used as in all other shots. Make sure on all shots that your buttocks stick out behind your heels as mine do in this picture. This gives you freedom of movement with your body and room for your arms and hands to work as you take your swing.

Everything starts together with the winding up of the body for the swing.

The neck is the hub of the wheel of action. The arms, hands and club are the spokes that are being revolved around the hub.

The shoulders have followed my hips around. With no suggestion of the wrists uncocking, the right elbow is still tucked
in to the right side and pointing down.

My wrists are starting to cock. My right arm is breaking and the right elbow is starting to point down as the club is taken back.

At the top of the swing note both my knees. The right knee is still flexed the same amount as at address. The left knee has bent in toward the right and has moved out only as much as the left hip has come around.

Starting down once again the initial movement is with the left hip turning to the left. My body action is being speeded up to pull the weight over to the left side for the downward blow.

Note that my right arm is tucked into the side, that the right leg is being relaxed and bending in toward the left. This enables me to hit from the inside out, the objective of every good golfer.

At impact my arms are still in the same relative position as at address, with the right arm lower than the left. With this setup I am able to take advantage of the loft of my club. If the right arm was out it would decrease the loft on the club as it met the ball, smothering the shot.

My arms and club are continuing on around the hub. The left hip has been moved on around to the left, giving the hands and arms ample room to pass through and complete the swing smoothly.

The right side is completely relaxed, the club is continuing
on up. At this point my shoulders have rotated and are pulling
the head up.

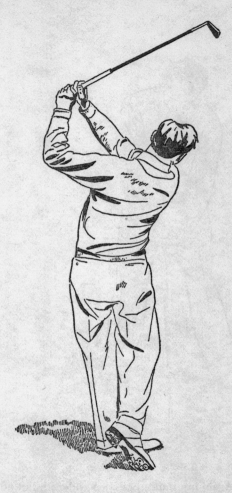

At the finish the pressure on my grip is the same as it was at address and all the way through the swing. If you relax the grip at the finish, you won't be aware of it, but actually this relaxing begins down at the ball.

Address. Again my stance has been widened, but not as wide as the stance used for a wood shot. The stance is also slightly closed. The purpose in widening the stance for the longer shot is for greater traction and more balance for the heftier blow. Note absence of strain here.

My backswing is underway here with a smooth rhythmical motion and with a full extension of the arms and hands. The body is coiling.

Note that my wrists are cocked later on this shot. The weight is being shifted to the right foot and there is more of a windup for the long iron shot than there is for the other iron shots.

The head is still stationary. The shoulders, arms, hands and club are being rotated smoothly around the hub as I make my swing.

My grip is firm throughout. As you approach the top of the
swing there is danger that you will allow your grip to loosen.
This can be costly.

The top of the swing. One of the so called "cross roads" of golf. The position here will almost determine a good or bad downswing.

Starting down. The objective is to create power and speed with the body before applying the arms and hands.

As is evident in this picture, you must have perfect balance before you can apply your strength and power in the right direction. Look where the clubhead is, almost back over my left shoulder, while my hands are midway between my waist and shoulders on the way down. This is brought about by delayed wrist action.

The weight has moved to the left side and I am all set for the hit.

It is quite evident in this picture that I have moved far enough on the left side to hit down and through the ball.

At impact my hands are ahead of the clubhead and the ball
is being struck a hard descending blow. Hit the ball first and
then take the turf.

Another impact shot. The pictures show three of these
shots. As they show unusual action I left them in for study. A
good study in this picture would be to note that from the
top of the left shoulder to the clubhead is almost a straight
line.

Almost a duplicate of the previous picture, this one shows that
my right hand has delivered a terrific blow at the moment
the ball was hit.

The hands have not started to pronate, or turn over, the face of the club is still square to the line of flight. Note the right foot.

The right side is relaxed, the hips turned around so that I face the direction of the ball flight. The shoulders, arms and hands are continuing their revolution around the hub as I complete the swing.

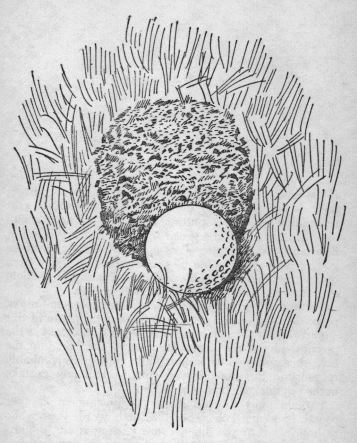

Divot. Here is a closeup of the divot taken by an iron shot. A ball has been placed in front of it in order to show you how far beyond the ball the divot should be cut by the club during the course of a shot. Never be afraid to bang down into the ball. Don't try to pick it off.

CHAPTER VII

Putting

FROM every observation I have ever made of putting there is no reason why the average player cannot putt reasonably well since putting is merely rolling the ball over the surface of the green by striking it a gentle but firm blow. Yet, in spite of its apparent simplicity, many golfers who are capable of playing excellent golf from tee to green have difficulty when faced with the problem of getting the ball into the hole with the putter.

Putting, it seems to me, is a matter of concentration, relaxation and confidence. Thus the mental phase of this department of the game looms at least as important as the physical phase, the actual stroking of the ball into the hole, because mental strain while putting is probably responsible for more missed strokes than any mistake in the physical mechanics of putting.

Par, on most courses, allows 36 putting strokes per round, two each hole. Therefore, it is worth your while to improve your putting because putting is one department of the game in which most of us can cut down on the number of our strokes by constant effort and practice.

You can lose a stroke on the fairway and have a chance to make it up before you are down, but a stroke lost on the green is lost forever. That is why putting, while apparently simple, assumes such importance in the game.

In order to be a successful putter you must adopt a sound approach and routine to that phase of the game.

136

Putting is the most individual department of golf. Once you have a smooth putting stroke a higher percentage of sinkable putts will start dropping for you regardless of whatever other individual idiosyncrasies you may have as a putter.

Putting has been the subject of a great deal of experimentation because of the possibility of reducing the number of putts to a round, but I shall concentrate here on the method of putting.

In my opinion the best grip to putt with is the reverse overlap grip. By that I mean that the index finger of the left hand overlaps the little finger of the right hand.

The reason I favor this grip in putting is that it permits you to have all of the fingers of the right hand on the shaft. That is because most of my putting is done with the right hand.

The left hand is under or to the left considerably in order that you may hinge your left wrist in comfort. It is the only way you can keep the clubface square to the line of the ball both going back and following through.

As I have said before, styles in putting vary and so do styles in stances and weight distribution. Most of the touring professionals, including myself, putt from a slightly opened stance. By that I mean that my right foot is ahead of the left foot. Almost all of my weight is on my left foot but my feet are not too far apart.

In addressing the ball let your body take up the position I have described in the chapter on stances. The tripod position, I have called it. It will assure you of perfect balance.

While putting I make sure not to move my shoulders, head or hips. I putt with my arms, hands and wrists.

Naturally, in addressing the ball your putter face must be at right angles to the line you have picked out for the ball to travel. The putter blade must remain at right angles during the stroke.

In stroking the ball take your putter straight back from the ball and straight through. Make sure that you hit through the ball on the finish.

Don't try to hit up on the ball to give it overspin. Concentrate on hitting it square, taking your putter straight back from the ball and straight through on the return stroke.

Once you have developed a sound putting stroke and can step up to putt relaxed and confident and with the ability to concentrate on the putting problem at hand, you are ready for a little advanced work in this department. The ability to concentrate carries with it the capacity to shut everything out of the mind except the golfing problem before you and how you are going to solve it.

This includes, of course, the selection of the proper line to the hole, the proper stance and grip and the correct estimate of how much power should be imparted to the stroke. Your ability to do all of those things in the proper sequence will give you confidence. It will permit you to relax and will leave you free of any tension or inner worry.

Most good putters have the ability to make their ball start rolling the moment it leaves contact with the club-head. This is imparted by the follow-through of the club and is something you feel when you stroke the ball perfectly. Let me say that it should be felt and not consciously thought about during the process of stroking the ball. The more roll you give the ball the farther it will travel in response to a stroke of given force. The distance you get depends upon power and roll.

You can develop this ability to impart roll to your putts by taking your putter home and practicing on the carpet. I've been taking a putter back to my hotel room with me evenings during tournaments for years and have found it worth while.

In getting ready to putt survey the over-all layout of the green in order to determine the amount of slope from side to side. Then survey the immediate area around the hole in order to have some knowledge of the amount of slope you will have to contend with when the ball is coming up on the hole. At the same time give some thought as to how fast you will have to make the ball travel in order to reach the hole.

Now stand behind the ball and view the line between

the ball and the hole. Whenever practical, size your putt up from the opposite direction.

This surveying and sizing up is all part of what is called "reading the greens." Much to my surprise, while talking with a friend recently I discovered that most duffers are amazed by the ability of the tournament professionals to "read the greens" on strange courses so quickly. By "reading the greens," of course, I mean the ability to look over the undulations, slopes and the grass on the putting greens and then decide how the ball is going to travel after you stroke it.

Bobby Locke, the South African, is the greatest putter I have ever seen. Bobby has a great putting stroke, but more than that he has an uncanny ability to read greens. I have never been to South Africa, but people who are familiar with the greens there tell me that they are very grainy. The reason that our greens held no terrors for Locke was his ability to read any kind of a green.

Naturally, this ability is developed only by experience, but there are certain little hints which I will give you which will help you to become proficient at it. If the tournament-playing professionals are more proficient at reading the greens than the ordinary player it is only because they have to play on so many different types of greens in the course of a year.

While they have never given me too much trouble I have been told that the greens are hard to read at Riviera in Los Angeles, site of the 1948 U.S. Open Championship. I won the 1947 and 1948 Los Angeles Opens there and the secret to putting well at Riviera is to locate the ocean in relation to the greens.

I am using Riviera as an example because it is a well-known course and because it offers a situation which is true at almost all oceanside courses. You can't always see the ocean at Riviera, but it is there nevertheless and has its effect on the roll of your putts on the greens. Everything breaks on the Riviera greens, and almost all oceanside course greens for that matter, toward the ocean.

When playing mountain courses, remember that putts will always break away from the mountains. This is true even if in "reading the greens" it doesn't look that way to you. Putting greens always slope away from the mountains on mountain courses because of the weather and erosion. What you will have to guard against in reading greens on mountain courses, however, is little things which your knowledge of golf will tell you can't be true, although they appear to be so to the naked eye. You'll learn what these things are only by experience and so I won't confuse you by trying to outline them here.

If you can locate the direction the grain of the green runs, you have won half the battle in your effort to get your putt down. One way of doing it is to look for the shine on the greens as you read them.

If you can see a shine on the green when you are lining up your putt it means that you are putting down the grain of the green. The ball is going to travel very fast. You will have to make allowances for the speed of the ball down the grain. Otherwise, if you make a mistake you will be sure to run by the hole several feet and will have another and even more difficult putt coming back against the grain.

When I see a shine on the grass on the right side in lining up a putt I play to the right even if I don't see a break in the green in that direction because I know the grain is running from right to left. The reverse is true if you see the shine on the left and you must then make your allowances accordingly.

If you are on the other side of the hole looking back toward your ball while trying to line it up and you see the shine, you will have to putt against the grain. When you putt against the grain it stands to reason you have to hit the ball a little harder to reach the hole.

Sometimes on a green you will find that the grain of the green breaks to the right while the roll and undulation of the green are to the left. When that happens you will have to decide whether you are going to play the grain or the roll.

Occasionally in this situation it is a good idea to play the ball straight in the hope that one will offset the other.

But that is something you must learn for yourself via the trial-and-error method.

You should also develop your ability to tell the kinds of grasses on the greens and their consistency through the feel of your feet on them as you walk around. Get so that you know the feel of the various grasses used on the greens and their relation to the speed of the ball, and that knowledge will be very helpful to you in learning how to putt.

Remember in putting that the stroke can't do it all. You have to know how hard to hit the ball and where to aim it.

Showing the side of my putting grip and illustrating that the back of my left hand is pointing toward the hole or line of the putt. If the palm of the right hand were open that would also be square with the ball. The grip in my left hand is entirely in the palm while in the right hand it is entirely in the fingers. Note the index finger and thumb of my right hand are my feelers.

The knuckle view of my hands clearly shows the reverse overlap grip used. In this the index finger of the left hand overlaps the little finger of the right hand.

Address. Take up a comfortable position regardless of how it looks. Have your eyes directly over the top of the clubhead. Make sure that the face of the putter is at right angles to the line you have picked.

Take the club back smoothly with the hands and arms, making sure that the clubface remains square to the line. Do not open or close the clubface on the backswing in putting.

At impact make a conscious effort to hit the ball squarely regardless of the distance. Do not try to hit up or down on a putt.

On the follow-through make sure that the face of the putter is square to the line. Do not open or close the clubface.

CHAPTER VIII

Bunker Shots Are Easy

PLAYING out of a bunker or trap became so easy for Gene Sarazen when he was competing in tournaments regularly that it was always suspected that he deliberately played into them when he was ahead in order to give the gallery the thrill of watching him get out. This is one of the easiest shots in golf, but most beginners are terrified at the idea of having to play out of a bunker. I can't understand why they should be because it is a shot which allows more of a margin of error than any other.

You don't even have to hit the ball on a short bunker shot. All you have to do is to hit the sand behind the ball. Of course, it must be done properly, but it isn't hard to do with the sand wedge we use today.

Let's discuss short bunker shots first. To simplify the short bunker shot use a sand wedge with as much flange as possible. The ideal club for this shot is a sand wedge of the type favored by the tournament professionals. The ordinary nine iron digs too deeply into the sand.

The sand wedge I mean is a heavy club, deeply lofted, with a large amount of clubface surface and a large flange which prevents the club from digging too deeply. If you use this kind of sand wedge start the shot with the idea in mind that you are going to let the club do the job. By that I mean that you are going to swing it, not scoop it. These clubs are so heavy that they will practically swing themselves if you let them.

On bunker shots assume the same tripod position you take on any other full swing shot. The stance, however, is opened considerably and your hips are facing to the left.

Make sure that you are loose and easy and under no obvious strain. It is very important, however, for your feet to be well anchored on this shot, otherwise they may slip in the sand.

Plant your feet firmly in the sand and then wiggle them around to make sure that you are solidly placed. While you are wiggling them around to secure good footing take notice of the firmness and texture of the sand. This knowledge will help you to decide how the shot should be played.

Of course, there is a penalty for touching the sand or *soling* the club at address, but aim approximately one inch back of the ball for most bunker shots. As you do this size up the terrain between the trap and the flag. If you can't see it from where you are standing at the ball take the time to climb out of the trap and look it over.

The clubface is open as you address the ball. Your hands are out in front. You are now ready to explode the ball out of the bunker or trap on all shots on which you can reach the green with the explosion shot.

In taking the club back on the backswing break your wrists early. The idea is to let the club come up fairly abruptly because it is necessary to hit down into the sand on the downswing until the clubface digs into the sand behind the ball. In spite of this, however, the bunker shot is made with a full swing, not a scoop, as the flange will prevent the clubface from digging into the sand too deeply.

As you break the wrists on the backswing, take the club back slightly on the outside of the line of flight you plan. Use a long backswing because it must make a smooth trajectory with the club, not a jerky one.

Start the club down from the top the same as on all other shots. The hips start turning first to bring you down into the hitting position. With the club on the outside hit down across the line, making sure that the clubface is open. The club bites into the sand approximately one inch behind the ball and goes on through to the finish with the clubface still open.

The follow-through is highly important. Crossing over the hands or closing the face of the club during this shot will cause you to shank. Shanking is one of the most serious errors in golf.

Obviously, this shot requires a firm grip. But in spite of that don't tighten up.

On long bunker shots the stance and the address are the same as on short bunker shots, but there are two other very important differences in the way the shot is played.

The first of these two differences is in club selection. On short bunker shots I advocated using the heavy sand wedge, but on long bunker shots the club used will depend on the length of the shot required.

A good rule to remember is to always take one more club than you would from the same distance on the fairway. Hitting the sand will deaden the shot just about one club, sometimes two. What the difference will be will depend on whether the sand is heavy or light.

It is a good idea to determine the consistency of the sand in the bunkers while you are wiggling your feet around to make sure of your footing, just as it was on short bunker shots. There are no tips I can give you about learning how to recognize the consistency of the sand and its effect on the shot, or I would. After you have played a few shots out of the sand you should begin to have some idea of how to judge whether the ball comes out slow or fast.

Your problem on long bunker shots is not only to get out of the bunker, but also to get as much distance as possible. When the tournament professionals find themselves 200 to 250 yards from the green in a bunker they will often play the shot with a four wood, but only when the lie is good. In using the four wood, or any other wood for that matter, out of a bunker make sure that you hit the ball, not the sand behind it.

That is the second of the two differences in the way

long and short bunker shots are played. Whether you use a wood or an iron you have to hit the ball first on long bunker shots in order to pick it up clean. I can't be too emphatic about this because it is very important on long bunker shots. As a consequence the ball has to be sitting up in the sand quite prominently before you can afford to take a chance with a wood club.

At address open the stance considerably, take about a quarter turn with your hips facing the hole. Open the face of the wedge, the hands are slightly in advance of the club, aiming approximately one inch back of the ball.

Start the club away from the ball smoothly a little on the outside of the line. Pick the clubhead up rapidly by breaking
your wrists early in the swing.

The wrists are broken to their maximum and make the complete backswing smooth and unhurried for all bunker shots.

I initiate the downswing again by turning the left hip to the left. Delay the hand action.

Make a conscious effort to hit down. Also make the downswing smooth and unhurried. It does not take a lot of strength or a hard swing to play this shot.

While hitting through the sand and on the finish make sure that the hands never turn over, or pronate. Keep the face of the club open.

Rear view of the address. Make sure that you are well set up in the sand as it offers tricky footing and you can't afford to lose your balance.

This picture shows that the club has been taken back on the outside and that the face of the club is still open at this stage of the swing.

Actually I cut across the line of the flight on this shot with the clubface open, making the club scoot through the sand so that it doesn't stick.

CHAPTER IX

Uphill and Downhill Shots

WHEN Bud Ward, two-time winner of the National Amateur Championship, was asked how he liked Carnoustie, the site of the 1947 British Amateur Championship, he said, "Every time I hit a great tee shot I found that I was playing my second shot with one foot up and the other foot down."

Of course, the Spokane amateur was referring to the fact that the hilly terrain at Carnoustie made it necessary for him to play his second shots from either downhill or uphill lies. While Carnoustie is an exceptional course, this is the kind of situation which will confront a novice more often than it will a finished player on the average course because the finished player can place his shots better than the novice.

A great deal has been written and said about ball placement on these kinds of shots, whether or not your left foot is high and your right foot low, or vice versa. Naturally, on a downhill lie the ball is back more toward the right foot than it normally would be. On an uphill lie the ball is more toward the left foot.

The reason for this in each case is to have the ball in the place where the lowest part of the swing will be. You will get the idea of how to play these shots more quickly by thinking of the relation of the ball to the arc of the swing rather than of whether to play it off one foot or the other.

When you have a sidehill lie and the ball is higher than your feet you play it farther away from the feet at address. As a consequence the arc of your swing is flattened by the position you have to take in relation to the ball. When you have a sidehill lie in which the ball is lower than the feet it must be played closer to the feet and the arc of the swing becomes more upright.

While the above is true it is not something you have to give a great deal of thought to as you play the shot. The change in the arc of the swing takes place automatically because of the lie of the ball and the way you have to swing in order to play the ball.

When you have your mind made up as to the position you want to play the ball from the next thing for you to do is to make up your mind as to what club you want to use. Before you decide that, however, make sure you have an accurate idea of the distance to the green. If you can't see the flag and green from your ball walk up the fairway to where you can.

In selecting the club to make downhill and uphill lie shots here are two things to keep in mind: When the ball is higher than your feet take one more club in range than you would if you were trying to make the same shot on the flat. When the ball is lower than your feet take one less club.

Reason: When the ball is higher than your feet you can't get as much power into the swing because your swing is shorter and you have to take about one more club in range to get the same distance. When the ball is lower than your feet the arc of your swing is lengthened and as a result you get more distance than you would making the same shot on the flat.

In selecting the club for loft remember that on a downhill lie you have to take a club with more loft in order to get the ball up into the air then you would making the same distance shot on the flat. You are already hitting down on the ball and need the additional loft to get the ball up into the air. For conversely the same reasons in selecting the loft of the club to play an uphill lie you need less loft than you would on the flat. You are already hitting up on the ball and don't require as much loft to get the ball into the air.

Regardless of the lie, whether uphill or downhill, or sidehill, I play the ball where the lowest part of my swing will be. Naturally, if the lie is downhill, as it is in this picture, I play the ball back farther toward my right foot because I know that is where the lowest part of my swing will be. On the follow-through I make an effort to make my club travel down with the slope of the hill.

On the uphill lie I play the ball farther up toward my left foot because that is where the lowest part of my swing will be. On the follow-through I make my club travel up, following the slope of the hill. On a downhill lie I always take more loft to get the ball up and on an uphill lie I take less loft to keep the ball down.

CHAPTER X

Stormy Weather Golf

MOST of us don't like to play golf when it is raining and stormy, but there are times when we are forced to play. For instance, when a rainstorm comes up and your opponent wants to keep on playing and you continue to play as an accommodation to him, or when you are playing in a club tournament and don't like to quit until directed to do so by the committee. On such occasions a knowledge of how to play under stormy weather conditions comes in very handy.

One of the most common errors made by golfers who have to play the game in wet weather is that they try to offset bad playing conditions by striving to attain their maximum capabilities, or even beyond, on every shot. They speed up the tempo of their swing in an effort to hit the ball harder and farther, but instead of overcoming the handicap they are playing under they usually increase their scores by a considerable number of strokes when it isn't necessary.

What you really should do when forced to play under bad weather conditions is to exercise restraint and play cautiously and well within yourself at all times. Care should be taken to hit the ball cleanly on all shots rather than the ground behind it.

If you should happen to hit the ground first, rather

163

than the ball, water will get between the face of the club and the ball and cause it to slide. When that happens you're apt to lose control of the ball at a critical time when the loss of a stroke or two will cause you serious trouble.

In taking up your stance make sure that you get firm footing. It is easy for your feet to slip in wet weather and an inopportune slip during the course of your swing could be disastrous.

Make sure that you get the ball up in the air. Tee your ball up slightly higher in order to be sure that you will hit it clean.

Take a little more time with your tee shots. Concentrate on hitting the fairway, even if you have to sacrifice distance by doing it. Playing out of the rough with any degree of accuracy or efficiency is next to impossible when it is wet.

Naturally, you're not going to get as much distance as you ordinarily do with either your wood clubs or your irons. Therefore, where you might be inclined to take a four iron for a shot under normal conditions, take a three iron to play the same shot in wet weather.

If you are forced to play a ball from a heavy, close lie, concentrate on getting it up in the air. Use a shorter range club because the ball will float anyhow. That is because in playing the ball out of the wet grass you're not going to be able to control the spin as well as if you were playing the same shot off dry grass.

Take very few chances. Don't try to cut corners. Invariably fairway wood shots and long iron shots take an unnatural flight off wet turf. For that reason play for the center of the greens instead of shooting dead for the pins when they are cut into the corners of the greens or hidden behind bunkers.

Furthermore, on a wet day you can throw away your brassie and one iron. It is almost impossible to get the proper flight on the ball with such straight-faced clubs.

Most trap shots have to be blasted out anyway, but particularly after the sand has been wet. It is the same kind of shot out of the trap in wet weather as it is in dry, except that you have to take a little heftier swing because of the heaviness of the sand.

Remember that the ball usually stops very close to where it lands on wet greens. You'll get practically no roll on your ball and will have to plan your strategy accordingly.

When playing golf during the time of the year when your section of the country is subject to sudden storms make sure that you are equipped to meet any emergency along those lines. Carry a sweater and light waterproof Windbreaker in your bag. Most of the tournament golfers carry this equipment, plus umbrellas. Umbrellas come in handy to keep you and your clubs dry while playing in the rain.

You should also be equipped with a towel or cloth to wipe your clubs and grips dry. Leather grips get slick and have to be wiped before each shot.

Many clubs are now equipped with an All Weather Grip which is made of cork, rubber and linen thread. They're very useful and enable you to get a good grip on your club no matter what weather conditions you're playing under.

Whatever you do, however, don't try to keep playing during an electrical storm. Conditions on golf courses are more dangerous than you realize and too many people playing golf have been struck by lightning and killed or seriously injured. Don't take any chances. Stop playing at once when an electrical storm comes up.

WIND SHOTS

There's an old saying in golf that when the wind blows the men are separated from the boys. It means, in so many words, that if you can golf when the wind is blowing you're a man; if not, you're still a boy.

Down in Texas the wind blows all of the time. That's why most of us golfers who learned the game there can play wind shots. If you can't maneuver the ball in the wind you'll never score well in Texas. Byron Nelson, Lloyd and Ray Mangrum, Ralph Guldahl, Henry Ransom, Harry Todd, and Jimmy Demaret are all great wind players. If they weren't nobody would ever have heard of them. They would still be down in Texas struggling to break seventy.

Of us all, however, I think Jimmy Demaret is the greatest wind shot player in the business. And men who have been watching tournament golf a lot longer than I have tell me that he is probably the greatest wind player the game has ever known.

All of which can be attributed to the fact that Demaret's first job as a professional was in Galveston, Texas, where strong winds blow in off the Gulf of Mexico day in and day out. Jimmy had his mind set on playing tournament golf even in those days and he spent all the time that he could working on his game.

During the course of the 1947 International Four Ball Championship at Miami, Florida, which Jimmy and I won for the second year in a row, Demaret made what I think was the greatest shot I have ever seen. The Four Ball was played at the Miami Country Club in 1947 and if you are familiar with the eleventh hole at that course you will recall how small the green is.

To complicate matters the wind was blowing strongly toward us out of the right quarter and the flag was cut in on the right side of the green. It was out of the question to hit a hook shot to the right and still keep the ball on the green as the wind would be sure to carry the ball off line.

After studying the situation for a moment Demaret hit the ball low into the wind and at the same time cut it to the right. It landed and stayed close to the pin.

Playing right along with Jimmy I could appreciate that shot because I was fully aware of the conditions he was playing under. Believe me, with the wind blowing as it was that day it was extremely difficult to keep the ball low and still reach the green. But by also cutting the ball to the right so that it landed close to the pin, Jimmy's shot approached the phenomenal.

I mention that particular shot not only to pay tribute to Demaret's ability in this phase of the game, but also to make you aware that it is possible to play golf in the wind and still control the ball. The idea, of course, is to play your shots, just as Demaret did that one, low into the wind at all times.

Quail high is the way we describe them in Texas. Keep the ball quail high and you will find yourself scoring better than the player who has plenty of power but is up in the clouds on every shot.

Any time you play golf on a windy day remember to widen your stance. Play the ball from a stance in which the ball is back more toward the right foot than you would ordinarily play it.

In addressing the ball, hood the face of your club just a little bit. Play your hands well in front of the club at address and also at contact.

Make sure you pick the club up more abruptly on the backswing, breaking the wrists to the maximum earlier in the swing than you ordinarily do.

Hit down into the ball more abruptly than you would on a regular shot, making sure that the hands are leading or drawing the swing and that the weight is well forward on the left foot. Try to keep the clubhead as low to the ground as possible on the finish. Don't let it come up immediately after contact. The hands should still be leading even while you are finishing up on the stroke after contacting the ball.

You will be surprised how little the wind will affect a low ball. Of course, when playing on a windy day you will have to favor the wind and take advantage of it. Make allowances for a certain amount of carry. Just how much carry to allow for, you can judge after playing a couple of shots. This is another good reason why you should warm up by hitting a few shots on the practice tee before starting a round of golf.

On windy days don't forget to play for a bounce and allow for quite a bit of roll. In playing a low shot to the green never try to carry the green unless it is necessary because of a bunker guarding it. In that case you will have to play a higher shot and make some allowance for the wind.

When playing against the wind be sure to use a stronger club than you would use for the same distance under normal conditions. Remember that the ball probably won't roll as much when you're playing against the wind and make allowances for that fact.

If you're playing with the wind use a weaker club than you would use under normal conditions. Make allowances for the fact that the wind will carry the ball and that you will probably get more roll than you ordinarily would on the same shot.

If the wind is blowing across the line of flight you are planning, take aim to the right or left of your objective, according to the strength of the wind and its likely effect on that particular shot.

Follow the above hints and take advantage of a windy day for an occasional session on the practice tee, and wind won't be the psychological hazard it was when you first encountered it.

CHAPTER XI

Now, It's Up to You

WHEN Willie Turnesa won the 1947 British Amateur Championship any number of golfers expressed surprise that he could do so well in a major championship when he had had so little chance to play competitive golf during the four years he was in the Navy. The answer is, of course, that once you have a good golf swing you will always be able to play good golf, provided you get a chance to practice sufficiently before engaging in competition.

Willie was able to regain his form very quickly once he began practicing because he has always had one of the best swings in the amateur ranks. His success is additional proof that it is worth while for a golfer to forget about his scoring while he is learning to play the game and to concentrate on developing his swing.

Once you have developed a good golf swing and acquired the knowledge of how to make the most of it nobody can take it away from you. Eventually you will be able to score well enough to make all the trouble you had acquiring a good swing worth while.

Golfers have been known to score well without ever learning how to swing correctly. Sooner or later, however, their game catches up with them and they're not able to shoot those good rounds any more. For instance, I know of one former winner of championship events who now has trouble breaking eighty. His unorthodox swing has caught up with him and it is now too late for him to start learning the game over again with any idea of making the most of it in tournament competition.

Bobby Jones still has the same sweet swing which characterized his game when he was the boy wonder of golf. Of course, he isn't as keen competitively as he was when he was the King of the Links, but he can still cut loose occasionally with a sub-par round or two, no matter how hot the competition may be.

The time to learn to groove your swing and organize your game is when you are on the practice tee. That's the place to start setting up the rhythm of each shot so that when you are confronted with the need to execute a similar shot during the course of a round you will automatically adopt the correct routine and rhythm without having to think about each step.

In using the word rhythm here I am not speaking entirely of the swing. The rhythm I have reference to here could also be described as *the order of procedure*. Walter Hagen was probably the greatest exponent of the kind of rhythm I have in mind to ever play golf.

Hagen took his own time doing things, but no one ever accused him of taking too much time during a round of golf. Walter might be late getting to the tee, but once he teed off he never wasted his own time or anyone else's.

When you practice go out on the tee with a purpose in mind, not just for exercise. You'll get the exercise anyhow and with a definite purpose in mind you will be adopting habits of concentration which will pay off when you actually play a round.

For instance, before you start allot yourself a definite time for practice. Plan in advance the kind of shots you are going to practice and how much time you are going to devote to each and stick to your schedule. I am a great believer in practice, but I am no longer able to spend as much time on the practice tee as I did when I first started playing tournament golf.

Speaking of practice, let me emphasize here that the golfers most in need of practice probably do the least. I have in mind the week-end golfers who, although they don't play enough to keep their muscles limber, go right out and start playing without warming up on the practice tee. As a contrast I don't know of a tournament golfer who would think of teeing off without warming up first, even for a practice round.

That's why, in most cases, even those week-end golfers familiar with the course score better on the back nine than they do on the front nine. It isn't that the back nine is any easier, they're just playing better because they have had a chance to warm up.

Sam Byrd, who played golf with Babe Ruth quite frequently while both were members of the famous New York Yankees, told me about a habit formed in baseball which Ruth brought over into the game of golf and which I think might well be adopted profitably by those who don't warm up on the practice tee before going out to play a round. I refer to Babe's habit of swinging two golf clubs while waiting his turn on the tee, just as he used to swing a couple of bats while waiting his turn at the plate.

Muscular freedom is probably more important in golf than in any other sport, but very few players take the trouble to get loosened up. My practice routine seldom varies. I start with the short clubs, usually a nine iron, and hit the ball easily.

Next take your eight iron and repeat the process. After which go up through your seven, six and five irons, increasing the length of your swing as the number on your club decreases.

In practicing with the wood clubs start in by using a spoon. Give yourself a good lie. It won't do any harm in this sort of practice if you tee the ball up. Use the driver last and only after you are satisfied with the results you have been getting from the other clubs.

Don't hit the ball at random. I pick out a spot in relation to the caddy each time and try to hit each shot exactly where I want it to go. While making the shot I consider the wind and any other factors prevailing that day and try to control every shot as if I were actually playing it during a round of a tournament.

While I am practicing I am also trying to develop my powers of concentration. I never just walk up and hit the ball. I decide in advance how I want to hit it and where I want it to go.

Try to shut out everything around you. Develop your ability to think only of how and where you want to hit the shot you are playing. If something disturbs my concentration while I am lining up a shot I start all over again.

An ability to concentrate for long periods of time while exposed to all sorts of distractions is invaluable in golf. Adopt the habit of concentrating to the exclusion of everything else while you are on the practice tee and you will find that you are automatically following the same routine while playing a round in competition.

Naturally, on the practice tee you don't get the variety of golfing problems you get in competition and it is more difficult to keep interested. My solution is to play each shot, as I told you before, as though it were part of an actual round.

For instance, one way in which I keep up my interest while practicing is by using my caddy as a target. I hit to the left of him, to the right of him and then I try to hit beyond him, planning each shot and repeating the process with each club. If the wind is blowing I try to play the ball into it so as to take advantage of it while still maintaining complete control of the ball. Try this routine and you will be surprised at how quickly it will help improve the command you have of each club. It also provides a good background of experience to draw upon in actual play.

While playing an actual round I sharpen up my concentrative powers and stimulate my interest in each shot by sizing it up as I walk up to where my ball lies. Make a habit of doing this and you will increase your powers of concentration threefold while also speeding up your play.

If you can't afford regular instruction one of the best methods of learning what constitutes good golfing form is to observe good golfers in action. At first the individual mannerisms of the players will cause their swings to appear different, but the important essentials will be identical.

Naturally, you have to have some idea of what to look for in advance when you watch these good golfers play in order to recognize it in rapid motion. For instance, all good players start the backswing back in a broad sweep. At first the head of the club will travel close to the ground. There is no suggestion that it is being picked up or lifted. In slow motion the action would appear to originate in the center of the player's body, and, following the turn of his hips, the club will be pushed back by the left side.

When watching the star golfers in action locate yourself at least part of the time behind them where you can easily see that the path of the clubhead never travels from the outside in. Unless the player is playing an intentional slice he will never allow his club to move out so far that it must approach the ball from outside of the line. Watch closely to see how this is made possible by initiating the downswing by the unwinding of the hips.

Note that good players don't throw the clubhead with the hands from the top of the swing, that their wrists remain cocked at almost the full angle until their hands have moved down approximately to the level of their waists. At the same time you will observe that the right elbow returns to the side of the body almost as soon as the downswing gets underway.

Check them and you will find that good players hold themselves up to the ball, that they never fall back on their right leg. As a result their clubs never come up abruptly after striking the ball. In every case the arc of the swing is flat near the bottom as the clubhead goes out toward the hole. If an iron is used the turf is taken from in front of the original location of the ball.

Rhythm being important to golf, note that all of the good players display a somewhat similar rhythm. They have a leisurely backswing, an unhurried start down and smooth acceleration of the clubhead speed right up to the moment of impact with the ball.

Naturally the most efficient way to improve your golf game is to take instructions from a competent professional. If you can afford it by all means take them, but give him a chance.

By that I mean sign up for a series of lessons rather than an occasional period of instruction. That's the way to convince your pro that you are serious in your desire to improve your game and are not just experimenting.

Listen to what your instructor has to say with an open mind. Don't bother to outline for him all the theories about the game you have acquired. He is probably more familiar with them than you are because, after all, golf is his business. Give him a chance to tell you his own ideas of how your game can be improved.

Probably the best way to make him acquainted with your game at the outset is to play a round of golf with him. However, have it understood that the round is to be considered as part of your series of lessons because golf is a business with him and it isn't fair to expect him to play a round with you for nothing.

Whatever you do, don't take a third party along when you go for your lessons. Your instructor is entitled to your undivided attention without the presence of a kibitzer who would only disturb your concentration.

No matter what your age may have been when you started playing golf, and no matter how long you have been playing, don't let anything discourage you from trying to improve your game. Anybody can become a good player. All you have to do is to give some thought to it and practice the fundamentals.

Don't take the attitude, like so many I know, "Oh, I'm too old to do that." You're never too old in this game. That's the beauty of golf. If you have keenness and determination there isn't anything you can't accomplish in this game.

MATCH PLAY GOLF

As a great many club championships and tournaments are decided by match play a few hints here on how to play match play golf might be helpful. Whatever you do, don't let your opponent's luck or skill influence you to change your style in an effort to catch up with him when he gets out in front. That is the first thing to remember about match play.

Your opponent may be just having a good day. The law of averages will catch up with him sooner or later. Don't overextend yourself in a vain effort to match him while he is hot. If you do you'll be sure to get in trouble. Before you know it you will have added strokes to your score which will prevent you from ever catching him.

Play your own game. Wait for him to make a mistake. When he does, and most golfers make mistakes sooner or later, try to take advantage of it.

For instance, in the finals of a very important championship my opponent had me three down at the end of the morning round. I knew I had to make a few birdies to stay in the match and catch him, but I didn't get upset when I couldn't seem to get them.

I knew that he was playing too perfect. He had to make a mistake sooner or later and that's what I waited for. Finally, on the second hole of the afternoon round he missed the green with his second shot and I was on it with mine.

That was my opportunity and I made the most of it. He bogeyed the hole and I won it with a par. There wasn't anything sensational about that kind of golf, but it seemed to upset him. Before he had steadied down again I had won three holes in a row to come from behind and take a one-up lead.

Naturally, that gave me a world of confidence. I eventually won the match and the championship. The point I want to make is: *Wait for an opening, don't force it.*

Of course, all of the above is only theory. Lots of times it won't work, but my experience is that more often it will.

When you are playing match play golf there is no reason why you can't use a little psychology on your opponent in an effort to defeat him.

For instance, if you and your opponent drive about the same distance let him outdrive you for once on a short par four. As you are away you will then have the honor of making your second shot. Your objective then should be to get the ball on the green as close to the pin as possible.

It has been proved that a ball sitting up close to the pin has a psychological effect on the fellow who has to make his second shot while his opponent's ball is on the green close to the cup. That's probably one reason why short hitters beat long hitters so often in match play championships.

The final of the 1938 Professional Golfers Championship, which was played at Shawnee-On-The-Delaware, probably offers the most famous example of a short hitter defeating a slugger. In that event Paul Runyan, a great competitor and not a long hitter, defeated Sam Snead, one of the longest hitters in the game, by the one-sided score of 8 and 7. Both Sam and Paul played well, but Paul was inside of Snead on the green quite frequently with his second shot in spite of being outdistanced off the tee. Paul's consistent ability to do that, plus his undeniable skill with a putter, enabled him to give Sam one of the worst beatings of his career.

If your opponent is on the green before you are, don't give up. You can be in a trap and still get down in fewer strokes. The reason I mention this is because so many fellows go about shooting in such a lackadaisical manner when they have to get on the green and down in one putt for a half. It can be done and has been quite often.

Walter Hagen had the greatest mental approach to golf of any player I ever knew. That is probably why he won the PGA Championship, which is decided by match play, five times.

Walter always thought that he was going to miss a certain number of shots a round. We could all profit from this example. Take the attitude that you are going to miss so many shots anyhow and then go ahead and play each hole for all that it is worth.

EIGHT HINTS ON HOW TO LOWER YOUR SCORE

1) *PRACTICE*. Almost always club members familiar with the course have a higher score on the front nine than they have on the back nine and the reason is that they are just getting "warmed up" when they play the back nine. If you will practice only as long as it will take you to hit five balls before you start it will help you to lower your score on the front nine. Furthermore, it is not just a case of "warming up" your muscles. You have to start thinking golf right from the start in order to score.

2) *COMMON SENSE*. Many players throw away strokes because they don't take the time to think about a shot before they attempt it. For instance, in playing over a bunker make sure to put your ball onto the green. Play your shot so as to make allowances for the margin of error to be on the far side of the cup rather than risk being short because of the danger of landing in the bunker. *USE YOUR COMMON SENSE*.

3) *USE A CLUB WITH ENOUGH LOFT*. A novice golfer is inclined to neglect to use enough loft when playing to the green. Consequently, he doesn't get the ball into the air high enough and is short. On the next hole the fact that he was short is fresh in his mind, but once again he takes the wrong club. This time he attempts to make an adjustment by hitting the ball too hard in seeking to insure himself enough distance. As a result his mistakes in club selection have cost him two strokes.

4) *PLAY SAFE IF YOU CAN'T GET A CLEAN SHOT*. Don't take any unnnecessary chances in the rough because you'll probably lose two or three strokes just trying to get the ball out. It is better to concede the loss of one stroke than it is to take a chance and sacrifice three or four.

5) *LEARN TO PLAY THE SAND WEDGE*. Most novices neglect to learn to use this club because they don't appreciate what a utility club it really is.

6) *LET YOUR CLUBS DO THE JOB*. Instead of trying to maneuver the ball with your body, arms and hands, trust your swing and the club you select to do the job.

7) *PLAY FOR THE GREEN, NOT THE PIN*. Never play for the pin when it is cut in a corner of the green that is severely bunkered. In this instance it is better for you to rely on your putting ability rather than your second shot. Take chances only after you have your game under control at all times.

8) *DON'T BE AFRAID*. Fear will influence your muscular reactions, so dismiss all ideas and fears of shooting over water off the tee at a green with water around it, or any other hazards. It is foolish to be frightened by hazards because most players have the club range to miss those hazards if they just swing freely.